MW01295175

VALUED

VALUED

The Six Coaching Habits that
*Turn **Subject Matter Experts** into*
Enthusiastic Talent Developers

MATTHEW J. DICKERSON

Niche Pressworks
Indianapolis, IN

VALUED

Copyright © 2024 by Matt Dickerson

All rights reserved. No part of this book may be used or reproduced in any manner whatsoever without prior written consent of the author, except as provided by the United States of America copyright law.

For permission to reprint portions of this content or bulk purchases, contact matt@mattdickersonvalued.com

Published by Niche Pressworks; NichePressworks.com
Indianapolis, IN

ISBN
Hardcover: 978-1-962956-02-4
Paperback: 978-1-962956-01-7
eBook: 978-1-962956-00-0

The views expressed herein are solely those of the author and do not necessarily reflect the views of the publisher.

*This is dedicated to the women in my life who,
at times, are forced to put up with me but,
in most cases, support my crazy ideas.
Thank you to Carrie, Abby, and Lily.
I love you and am thankful for you.*

TABLE OF CONTENTS

FOREWORD

Yes, it's often a bumpy road, the path to effectively leading others. As Matt Dickerson points out in his description of the six habits of successful coaches, the journey of becoming a competent, exemplary leader is usually not a straight-line endeavor. There are seminal moments when a young leader decides that they really enjoy leading others and are pretty good at it, or they decide that they prefer to stay in roles primarily focused on being individual performers.

He aptly describes his own journey and explores the idea that "leadership and coaching others is not just a means to an end but rather an overarching aspect of work that can bring you better alignment with your own core values."

This resonates with me for two primary reasons. First, I had the privilege of working in a well-functioning business environment for over twenty-five years and saw first-hand the benefits and power of having leaders who were passionate about developing others while delivering results for the organization. Some individual performers wanted no part of managing others, self-selecting out of that "emerging leader" category, while others found immense rewards and satisfaction along the sometimes-messy journey. One key to that choice is described nicely by Matt in the chapters that follow as "... a deep sense of self-knowledge [that] allows you to show up confidently for others in the way that meets their needs, at that moment in time." You serve as the coach, the sounding board they need you to be. Matt details the process and tactics that enable a leader to "meet their people where they are" and do it in an authentic manner.

In a highly technically connected world that is not hierarchical, we cannot assume that only those with title or authority play leadership roles. Each team member needs to be able to step up at certain times to lead the project or coach others on the team. Our field research and writing relative to *The Catalyst Effect* (Emerald Publishing, 2018) support the idea that "you lead from wherever you are," regardless of title or authority. The virtual work environment and project team methods of getting work done demand that each of us is able to step up when needed.

What Matt points out nicely in his description of the six habits of successful coaches is that the challenging road of becoming an exemplary leader who is able to coach others can be highly rewarding. The six habits clearly describe the necessary mindset and skills that leaders (whether formal or informal) need in order to be effective. I hope you enjoy reading this book as much as I did. It is sprinkled with personal examples and coaching concepts that will encourage your own thinking about how you can become the best coach you can be as we each make our way down the "bumpy road."

— **Jerry Toomer,** author of *The Catalyst Effect*

PREFACE

> For me, inspiration is something that happens just below the level
> of consciousness and is easier to pinpoint in retrospect.
> — Omer Fast

It's no secret that our occupations require a significant amount of our time, energy, focus, and effort. It is also true for many of us that our work is a substantial driver of our self-perception. Hundreds of books are published every year with lessons meant to help us grow, achieve, succeed, thrive, or simply get by in extreme workplace situations.

These offerings speak to a culture that espouses that self-efficacy is the only driver of relative performance and that you are solely responsible for your success. In other words, if you are self-driven and if you can adopt these best practices or this particular mental model, you can achieve.

While your role in your own development is important, what is not given as much light is the notion that we are responsible for others' development. This is especially true when someone holds a position with people management responsibilities.

I had a boss tell me that, in their opinion, a young professional would be less likely to advance in an organization unless they (1) moved or traveled often *or* (2) managed people at multiple points in their career. My bet is that you have heard something similar or have felt that to be true at some point in your career.

In this book, the distinction will be made between manager/director/team lead and leader. We will intentionally use the term "leader" to refer to one who others follow. While I am standing on the shoulders of many great authors and researchers in this distinction, it is an important one to delineate here.

Managers have well-documented duties and are responsible for overseeing a group of people and their execution of tasks. They handle administrative responsibilities and often serve as conduits of information between management above them and those who report to them.

Leaders, as inferred by the name itself, promote an environment where people follow their lead. Followers don't follow people who are absent of vision. Further, followers don't follow unless they are convinced that following will have benefits for them.

Most critically, followers follow those they believe truly care about them and their professional goals.

Most critically, followers follow those they believe truly care about them and their professional goals.

So why is it that so many leaders and leadership experts espouse that trust is built through expecting those you lead to be self-sufficient? What makes people leaders expect those they lead to demonstrate self-efficacy and find a path on their own?

I've heard this sentiment too often, both from peers and clients I coach.

And to some extent, these ideas are not completely inappropriate. It would not be prudent for a leader to spend extra time on someone's development if they are not fully invested in their own growth. Our time and energy are limited, and, as leaders, we shouldn't be "throwing good money after bad." If they are not interested in progressing their career or growing their skill, there is little a leader can do to motivate or inspire action.

However, if they are motivated, they usually need help. As we'll discuss, they might not know what to ask for.

I am thankful for the opportunities I have had over the past two-plus decades to experiment, fail, learn, and grow. I have led people formally for more than fifteen years at different organizations. I am also a certified coach and have used many of the tools and tactics I discuss in these pages.

I have NOT achieved mastery in any of the topics I discuss. I write and share out of a desire to contribute to the development of the leaders and potential leaders who might read it. My hope is that some of the connections I make will inspire others to lead better — to invest more *proactively* into the people they are attempting to lead.

Writing this book also gave me the opportunity to survey other leaders for their opinions and experience. This research should not be viewed as scientific but rather as informative. The several dozen respondents gave countless stories of what good and bad leadership has looked like for them in their careers. The statistics derived from their responses and the accompanying stories will be sprinkled throughout the chapters to come.

In this book, we will learn about six coaching habits that will increase your effectiveness in leading people. We will define the habit itself using helpful examples and stories. We will also review what that habit is seen as — how you show up if you are demonstrating that habit. And finally, each habit is associated with a value or belief. You can think of this as the mantra you might repeat to yourself as reinforcement or focus.

You've probably worked for leaders of varied skill levels. The best among them — the heroes in your own story — understood infinitely more about you and your development than you did or could be expected to. They knew about the tools that were available for your development. They understood your company's culture and how to direct you in navigating it for mutual benefit. They had the wisdom of experience and what is possible.

And here's the key: The best leaders out there know that *they* must be the ones to share that wisdom. They know their team members do not know all the right questions to ask. They know we can't possibly have a vision of a path we have never taken. They implore their people to hold them accountable for making *others'* development *their* priority.

They *thrive* in the responsibility to proactively teach and guide others. Let's explore together what that might look and feel like and how you might walk in the footsteps of the great people developers who went before you.

> *It's really easy to insist that people read the manual. It's really easy to blame the user/student/prospect/customer for not trying hard, for being too stupid to get it, or for not caring enough to pay attention. ... But none of this is helpful.*
> — **Seth Godin**, Tribes

CHAPTER 1

WHAT IS LEADERSHIP?

> Life is short, and there is not much time for us to
> gladden the hearts of those who travel the way with us;
> so be quick to love; and make haste to be kind.
> — Henri-Frédéric Amiel

CARLOS AND MISUNDERSTANDING LEADERSHIP

Carlos knocked on his boss's door. "Hey, Sandra, you wanted to see me?"

"Yes, come on in!"

As Carlos closed the door behind him and sat at the table in Sandra's office, he knew why he was there. Carlos was a 30-something expert in his field. He had excelled in his industry and demonstrated loyalty to his company. He knew he was capable of more and was excited to see that happen. The issue was he was starting to feel like he was hitting a ceiling. What more could he accomplish in his current role? How could he keep challenging himself and making progress in his career? Did he have to manage people in order to advance, or could he find a new assignment where he could just focus on his own work?

After offering Carlos a bottle of water, Sandra began. "I know I tell you often, but you are incredible. I was reminded again just last week by the way that you led the team to meet an impossible customer deadline."

He nodded as if to say, "Thanks."

She continued, "But we both know you need a new challenge. You've done all you can on this team."

While he agreed, he dreaded what was coming.

He tried to get out in front of it. "Thanks, Sandra. I appreciate the kind words. Your support has always meant a lot to me, and I'm proud of the work we've done. I am feeling a bit restless, but I don't know what's next. I'm pretty sure I don't want to manage anyone. That doesn't leave me with a lot of opportunities. But I also don't have a lot of interest in exploring roles at other companies. I love it here!"

Sandra smiled. "What concerns you about leading a team?" (She was great at asking good questions.) "You would be great!"

Carlos responded carefully but firmly. "We've gone over this in the past. I like being in charge of me!"

Sandra listened patiently (she was good at listening, too).

He joked, "Can you guarantee that everyone on my team puts in as much effort as I do? Can you match me with a team with no duds?"

She laughed along, knowing that his joke underscored a real concern for him.

He continued, "I just have no interest in a role where I have to babysit adults. I can't even imagine the crap you have to put up with on a day-to-day basis. And you're great at it! Holding low-performers accountable, getting in between us and upper management, and hearing all the sob stories and excuses. And the whole time, *you're* being evaluated on *their* work. No thanks. I want to be known for what I can do."

He took a breath.

Sandra knew this was an important moment in a critical conversation.

"You're right. Some of my day-to-day is that. But what about the good stuff?"

Okay. Carlos knew that Sandra could ask some good questions, but this one seemed silly.

"Good stuff?" he probed.

"Do you think all I do all day is sit through meetings, push paper, and yell at people?" Her question had not a hint of judgment or criticism. Watching his face, she sensed an opening — an opportunity to expand his thinking. She continued.

"Do you remember last year when you approached me about the new idea you had for the Ferguson project?"

"Of course," he said. "I was excited that you were open to what I was thinking. We had a great conversation, and I knew we'd hit on something new and special."

"How did you feel leaving the conversation?" she inquired.

"I felt like you were really listening to me and that you were allowing me some freedom to be creative. I left feeling empowered and pumped up about what was possible."

"Would you like to know what I was feeling?" she asked.

It's funny; he hadn't given much thought to what she might have been feeling. Don't misunderstand; this was just another instance he was glad to work for who he worked for.

He just hadn't stopped to think about what *she* might have gotten out of the encounter.

"Sure," was all he could muster.

"I felt incredible!"

He hadn't expected that.

As she continued, Carlos could tell that she was really opening up.

"Those are the moments that remind me that I am where I need to be. I couldn't fall asleep that night." Sensing Carlos wasn't totally buying in, she quickly added, "I am not exaggerating."

As she continued to share, Carlos uncovered thoughts and feelings about leadership he had yet to consider.

"I discovered years ago that I hold a core belief that I need to be providing value — value in my relationships, value in my marriage, value in my community, value in my career, value to my coworkers. You might say that providing value is a core value for me. Do you know what happened in that moment?" she asked without pausing for an answer. "I had aligned my career — my role responsibilities with my core values. And it couldn't have happened without you!"

She had his attention.

"I knew, in that moment, that I had met *your* need and equipped you in a way that would have been easy for me to miss. I could predict your success and the satisfaction you would derive from it. I knew I was fulfilling my purpose. And ... equipping yours."

Carlos was trying to process.

"Does that sound like babysitting adults?" she asked with a smile.

Carlos was processing. "I like to see others succeed. But what if I don't get that same kind of joy from it? What if it doesn't mean that much to me? What if I'm just not made like that?"

"Fair questions," she conceded. "But have you stopped to consider?"

He hadn't. Have you?

THE RUB

One problem, maybe the most obvious, is that many high performers avoid formal leadership opportunities because they underestimate what's in it for them. And that decision is made with incomplete information. The brutal truth is that, in most business environments, this is likely inhibiting their growth and promotion opportunities.

Perhaps the less obvious concern is that they would be missing an amazing opportunity to find fulfillment in the work — alignment between professional goals and core values. They may be missing the very thing they are looking for in their career: purpose.

Because of their preconceived notions of what management is and isn't, they are effectively eliminating what could be the Holy Grail of professional satisfaction.

It is not that all high-performing people will *definitely* value leading others in a formal management position or that they can all be good at and gain benefit from leading people.

The problem is that, because they have incomplete information, their decision about leading people has been premature.

> **The problem is that, because they have incomplete information, their decision about leading people has been premature.**

They are opting out, believing they have an idea of what managing people is and isn't. They have withdrawn themselves from consideration before they fully understand the riches investing in others might produce. For other people. For them. For them *because* it's for other people.

A TRANSFORMATIVE LEADERSHIP EXPERIENCE

Early in my leadership journey, I was leaning into the development of a high-potential team member. We'll call him Trent for the purpose of this story.

Trent was interested in moving up in the organization. He'd been in sales for about ten years and was eager to stretch into a new role. At the time, he had two positions he could reasonably work toward. One was to manage a team of his peers, and the other was a contributor role where he would call on larger customers. Either would be a promotion and an opportunity to stretch himself in new ways.

After several conversations, he elected to pursue the manager position. Our company made significant training available to him, and he diligently navigated the content. Intellectually, he had no problem picking up concepts and frameworks. He was a really smart guy.

But something wasn't clicking for him when he attempted to model the tactics he was learning.

I had to make the tough call. I knew this guy needed more challenge in his job. I knew our company would benefit from him being in a role with more scope and impact. Ultimately, I believed he would be better suited in the short term for the role with no formal people leader responsibilities.

This would also provide an amazing opportunity to see how managers in our organization interacted with their peers and teams. As an account manager, he would be responsible for directing other individual contributors in their interactions with large customers but not have any direct report responsibilities — otherwise known as a "dotted line" relationship. He would work with people managers like me and directly observe how I supported people and held them accountable. This role would serve as part of his development toward future people leadership, as he took note of what he might do similarly or differently.

Meanwhile, we needed to remove him from the training program and adjust his learning.

While I would have preferred to discuss this in person, it wasn't possible, so I gave him a call. I praised him for his work so far while also relaying the news that a different path would be best for him.

He didn't agree.

He paused, and I pictured him taking a deep breath and mustering up the most composure he could. "I don't agree with this decision," he said carefully. "I think I would make an excellent manager." He took another breath and continued, "I guess I just don't understand. I thought I was doing well in the training program and that you supported me in this process." He clearly didn't agree with my assessment. We could probably make a few assumptions about some of the emotions he was experiencing.

I gave some space for his comments and responded gently but firmly, "I can appreciate what you're saying. You immersed yourself in the training program, and I commend you on the effort you put forth over the past six months or so." I took another pause. "Based on how you're developing, I believe it's going to take you more time to be fully equipped to lead people well. In the meantime, I believe you could be quickly ready for the next challenge in a manager role that has no direct reports."

I stretched my luck and made one last point, "It's also likely that positions like these would open more quickly than one leading a team." (My actual words were probably not this concise or well-spoken, but this reflects my sentiment.)

After hearing me out, he said something to the effect of, "I don't want to be rude, but I think I need some time to think about this. I worry that I might say the wrong thing if we keep talking."

I could understand and was glad to allow him the time he requested.

After some time to reflect and process, he came to accept the direction I was advising. When we spoke next, he said, "I have to be honest. I still think I could be a good manager in the short term. However, I am motivated to take a next step and would like to get to work on our revised plan. What's next?"

I had, and have, a huge amount of respect for how Trent showed up in this moment. In my experience, he approached everything with this kind of class and integrity.

We doubled down on his development toward this new sales position. I helped him build a plan for learning specific skills. I committed to helping him make networking connections. He pursued the plan with diligence and consistency. He was creating his internal brand, and the people he interacted with were impressed.

And then, when a position came open nearby, he was one of eight people who applied for the promotion.

The hiring director called me two weeks later to let me know that his next call was to Trent to offer him the role. I hung up the phone and shed a tear. It was as if I had just been promoted!

Trent and I caught up shortly thereafter. He was appropriately excited and had gladly accepted. He said, "You remember that call we had when you said I was being removed from the manager training program?" I nervously chuckled and said, "Yeah."

Trent said, "I was really mad at you. I was trying to be professional, but I felt like you were underestimating me." And then he said something I will never forget:

"I get it now. Looking back on the last six months, I get it now. Only from this perspective can I see how much you were looking out for me in that moment. I couldn't see the plan. This wouldn't have been possible if we hadn't narrowed our focus on my development the way we did. Thank you."

Phew. It's been years, and I still get emotional recounting the story here.

That kind of fulfillment isn't possible if success only benefits you. Those moments create a meaningful professional journey — one with meaning and purpose.

The following chapters explore the possibilities along that journey. I make the case that not only is it possible for people like Carlos to be promoted into a people leadership role, but they can also (1) excel in that role with the right tools and mindset, (2) have a hugely beneficial influence on those they lead, and (3) find lifelong, values-aligned professional satisfaction.

If you've read this far and you want to keep reading, you might be experiencing your own fork in the road. What causes you to reflect on this topic? Is it, "I can't advance without managing people, but I'm unsure that's what I want"? Is it, "I've always thought of myself as a more informal leader. I value sharing my experience, but dread the 'dark side' of managing imperfect people"? Or is it, "I question whether or not I have the requisite skills or passion to invest in this type of work"?

Or maybe you're already faced with managing people, and you're just trying to get the most out of that experience.

All of you are welcome here. My sincere hope is that you find inspiration and ideas from what follows.

CHAPTER 2

WHEN I GOT IT WRONG...

> If I can't change the world, then maybe I can at least
> change something about the space in the world,
> the instruments in the world.
> — Vito Acconci

THE FIRST TIME

Let me tell you a bit about my bumpy path to managing people and *finding value from it.*

I worked for a bank while in college, which led to a role at a large national financial institution once I graduated. I was offered a position in their management training program and quickly assumed management duties.

After completing the program, I became an assistant branch manager and was on my career path!

It was an established branch in a very old neighborhood. Many of the employees had been there ten-plus years and had seen many changes, including the bank's name, through mergers and acquisitions. I was a doer. I took on projects like cleaning up files and reorganizing our storage, as well as logistical tasks like ordering supplies. I also provided structure to their processes.

I was establishing trust with the staff and had even been able to run interference between them and a branch manager who was out of touch, at best.

And I didn't like it. It was tedious. I had to fill in for my team members when they called off sick or simply didn't show up. I had to cover for them when they underperformed on new initiatives we were given. I held their hands on the smallest of tasks and had to train and retrain constantly.

And the constant monitoring of their activities — ugh!

It came to a head one week. I oversaw an employee who I thought had a heart of gold and a decent work ethic but who was often discussing her dire financial situation. Her salary at the bank, combined with her husband's spotty work, meant that they had to provide for a family at wages below the poverty line.

And then, I stumbled on some unusual transaction activity on her personal accounts and the terminal she oversaw.

I ordered some research out of a duty to explore further. When the copies came through the interoffice mail, she was the proactive person who opened the envelope.

She came to my desk.

"Did you request this?"

"Uh, yes," I stammered.

"You thought I was doing something wrong? Did you think I was stealing money?" she asked incredulously.

"I wasn't sure, so I had to check," I was able to force out.

As she began to tear up and turn to walk away, I thought, "What am I doing?"

I had an incompetent manager, a low-performing and needy team, and now I had alienated one of the few on my team who actually worked hard. I lost her trust and our ability to rely on each other. Spoiler alert: she wasn't doing anything wrong. Her crime was moving money between her accounts, which did not meet *my* definition of normal money management.

All I wanted to do was experience professional success. I had worked hard to gain this role and had a vision of a future career filled with achievement and accomplishment.

If managing people was just about micromanaging the smallest of tasks and occasionally getting it very wrong, this was not the role for me.

I didn't need the headache of managing people to get there. I had confidence in myself and preferred to work alone or as a member of a team. I didn't need to lead to get where I wanted to go.

I was wrong about all of it.

Looking back, I would be hard-pressed to find something I was gladder to be wrong about.

Let's fast-forward about ten years or so.

A SECOND TIME ... IN A NEW WAY

It was all great ... until it wasn't.

After several years as an individual salesperson in three different companies, I was presented with an opportunity to manage people again. I still had scars from my last experience. I was nervous about the opportunity to manage people, but I knew it was likely to happen again. Based on my previous experience, I thought I could be *somewhat* good at it, although I would doubt that — and myself — several times during my training and development. Still, I had learned things from my failures at the bank, and I'd worked for several leaders with varying skill levels. I could learn from them and find success.

And success came. When I was given the chance to manage a high-performing sales team in my early thirties, we experienced immediate success. In our first year as a team, we won several sales awards. More awards followed in subsequent years, and members of my team were achieving their career goals, including sales success and career advancement.

It was generally known that I was the beneficiary of a great business environment, fantastic peer managers to lead our large customer success, and a team of very high-performing individual sales representatives.

I was also given a lot of credit for developing the people on my team. I was motivated to mentor and coach where I could. I was eager to share new ideas and best practices with and between team members. I was equipped for tough conversations and willing to confront whenever necessary. I held people accountable. And as people moved on, I was fortunate to find more talented people to add to my team.

My heart was in the right place, and things were working. Except, it wasn't going to last.

As a results-oriented, extroverted leader, I responded best to those who approached their work with a similar attitude. We were largely a team of hard-driving, type-A personalities who liked to talk and be heard. I led a team that largely looked, acted, and sounded like me.

I was missing an appreciation for diversity in every sense. My team was overwhelmingly white, heterosexual, and male. Less obvious, they were also goal-oriented, data-over-people decision-makers who valued accomplishing much and contemplating little. I completely discounted ways of achieving success that varied from my preconceived ideas of what great looks like.

More reflective voices were simply not heard. I lament the instances where dissenting opinions or varied approaches could have provided more creative ideas.

I recognized then I needed to be much more intentional about learning things about inclusion, too. I was not aware of how ill-equipped I was until I started reading more about diversity, equity, and inclusion. Needless to say, I still have a lot to learn.

In *Inclusion on Purpose: An Intersectional Approach to Creating a Culture of Belonging at Work*, Ruchika Tulshyan makes countless important points. This one aligns most closely with the intent of this book:

"I am convinced that inclusion is the most important leadership trait today. If we define leadership as the ability to influence and inspire others to action, we'll notice that for far too long, we have lauded white male leaders for grooming, inspiring, and propelling the next generation of leaders like them. We need to change this paradigm urgently so that everyone with ambition, skill, and potential can succeed."[1]

At the same time, I was judging my success on external markers like sales success, awards, and promotions, which all suggested that I was leading well, investing in others, and achieving success that would support my ongoing career goals. I failed to understand the impact of my narrow brand of leadership.

What was missing was the greatest part of leading people — connection to all types of talented people.

> **What was missing was the greatest part of leading people — connection to all types of talented people.**

The first turning point: My company provided me with the amazing opportunity to train as a certified coach, and I'd been implementing that training internally. That process taught me a lot about myself and the ways in which I showed up to others (good and bad).

I learned that my brand of leadership was greatly influenced by my own core values but that I still had work to do to identify those values. I discovered that I talk *way* too much and ask too few questions. I uncovered that I had way more insecurities and questions than I had the wisdom to share. What's more, I learned that I didn't need to have the answers!

The second turning point: I accepted a project management role and failed to accomplish the objectives. I swung the pendulum all the way over to the other side. Instead of dictating next steps and "transferring my knowledge" to my colleagues in the projects, I asked thoughtful (I hoped) questions and left conversations open-ended. While it may have been closer to the inclusive environment I'd come to revere, I did not provide sufficient direction and clarity, and the progress of the project suffered.

Through that series of missteps and failures in a fifteen-month assignment that took me away from my primary team, I eventually returned as a humbled yet eager leader.

What I found on my return was a more diverse team ready to provide me with some lessons in leadership. I discovered a way to lead that was more aligned with my core values and much more respectful of the people I was tasked to lead.

I discovered my professional purpose in life: devoting myself to the development and advancement of others. I realized that leading people was not a means to an end; it was the beautiful destination I sought.

> **Leading people was not a means to an end; it was the beautiful destination I sought.**

FOR THE READER

If you're reading this, you likely fall into one of a few categories:

- You might be a high-performing employee who is being asked to lead people, but you're hesitant to be tasked with "babysitting" adults.

- Maybe you're currently seeking a promotion to a people leadership role but are unsure about that path. You might be very confident in your content knowledge. You might be even more assured of your ability to achieve as a member of the team. Maybe you have doubts about your willingness or your ability to manage others.
- Perhaps you have a long history of success as an individual contributor and long ago ruled out managing others.

Regardless of which of these is most true for you, you might also be searching for meaning in your career and have yet to find it. What is your professional purpose? How can you provide value to whatever company you decide to attach yourself to? How can *you* be valuable to others and be valued by them?

This book explores your potential purpose — how to align your core values to the work that you do through leading other people well. How will you become valuable to your team and your organization while gaining professional fulfillment for yourself?

SIX COACHING HABITS OF TALENT DEVELOPERS

 Coaching Habit #1
FOCUSING ON OTHERS

 Coaching Habit #2
RECOGNIZING WHAT'S NEEDED OF YOU

 Coaching Habit #3
BEING INTENTIONALLY PROACTIVE

 Coaching Habit #4
MODELING GROWTH

 Coaching Habit #5
REFLECTING AND ACKNOWLEDGING

 Coaching Habit #6
DRIVING RESULTS

CHAPTER 3

COACHING HABIT #1
FOCUSING ON OTHERS

Habit Is Seen As: Curious and Caring
Value or Belief Behind This Habit: It's About Them

If you're reading this book, you are likely a high-performing person in your professional life. People have different paths to success, but there are often some common traits, especially early in one's career. You might identify with many of the following: hard-working, driven, results-oriented, caring, loyal, intelligent, committed, collaborative. The list could go on.

But:

- How often do you consider what another person in your sphere of influence really needs?
- How often do you ask questions instead of making statements?

- How often do you demonstrate curiosity and caring with and for others?

The first and most foundational coaching habit is *focusing on others*.

We are fundamentally wired to be most concerned about what is in our best interest. This isn't inherently selfish. It is survival. It is also true that we are the people we think about the most and of whom we have the most knowledge. So, it's natural to be thinking about what we want, need, and are concerned about.

And ... evolution to great people leadership often starts with this paradigm shift to focusing on others. In order to accomplish what we want to accomplish, we need others. Accomplishment includes promotions, project or sales success, accolades, and awards. It also includes finding self-satisfaction and self-fulfillment in our careers.

Results from the survey I sent out support the "why" behind this coaching habit.

For example, roughly half of all respondents (~48%) rated *empathy* **as** the most important attribute or competency in a leader. Nearly two-thirds (64%) rated it in their top three attributes/competencies. Empathy starts with taking the focus away from yourself and putting your attention on someone else.

YOU KNOW SOMEONE

You probably know someone in your professional or personal life who is really good at this.

It's possible they were just built this way. As we'll dive into in Chapter 4 (Coaching Habit #2 – Recognizing What's

Needed of You), personality tendencies can show up here, too. Some personality styles are naturally prone to making the conversation, event, or topic about someone else.

It could also be possible that the others-focused person you are thinking of spent time and energy dialing up their empathetic, listening nature in order to be more effective either in their career or personal life or both.

Being exceptional in this habit is not limited to those who come by it naturally. It is very true that this habit can be learned. We will explore more here.

 COACHING HABIT #1 - FOCUSING ON OTHERS

HABIT IS SEEN AS: CURIOUS AND CARING
VALUE OR BELIEF BEHIND THIS HABIT: IT'S ABOUT THEM

HOW DOES SOMEONE SHOW UP AS CURIOUS AND CARING?

Knowing and understanding more about each other's tendencies and preferences is a great step in this direction. As mentioned, we will go into more detail about assessments in Chapter 4 (Coaching Habit #2 – Recognizing What's Needed of You).

It also takes intention You must do the work in preparation. You must be present in the moment, when you're interacting. We'll explore being present in a future chapter.

For now, let's focus our attention on something basic and practical — something very hard for many of us: asking good questions. Let's walk through what that might look and sound like.

Years of helping to solve problems have taught me that when you listen effectively and empathetically, it shows you care. And until people believe you care, they won't fully engage with you.
— **Andrew Sobel and Jerold Panas**, Power Questions

ASKING MORE QUESTIONS THAN MAKING STATEMENTS

Start asking questions!

I used to be *terrible* at this! My motivation to help, my ego about what I knew, or simply the fact that I liked to talk, often got in the way of asking good questions.

What's at stake?

If you're making more statements than asking questions, possible costs include:

- Repeating things the other person already knows
- Misunderstanding the nature of their interest or concern or question and taking the conversation in a way that is less productive
- Leaving them with an impression of being unheard, underappreciated, not well-understood, or even demeaned (they hear, "You obviously don't know much about this topic, so let me inform you")
- Demonstrating a lack of interest in their view/position

The survey results allude to the importance of this approach, too, as the single highest-rated attribute/competency was *listening*.

Ed, a former successful senior leader and current author, speaker, and coach, shared this unfortunate story about how destructive telling versus asking can actually be:

> "I had been working for a leader that I liked and ad-mired when I got a call from him to say he was moving into a new role, and I would have a new boss. After joining the company, the new boss called to tell me he wanted to fly into Atlanta and meet with me. His sched-ule only permitted him to be in town for a few hours.
>
> "When he arrived at the office, we retreated to a conference room, and he began to describe how he worked and how he expected me to work. He never asked me for my input or asked me any ques-tions about me — in other words, he didn't bother to get to know me at all. He came in on a mission to extol his methods, and he delivered. When he fin-ished his talk, which was at least an hour, he then asked me, 'What do you think?' I immediately re-plied, 'You sound like a used car salesman!'
>
> "Needless to say, he and I didn't get along from that point forward ... The first opportunity I could, I found another role with another com-pany, which led me to the best years of my career."

How often do we put limits on what we are willing to hear? "We can discuss *these* options, but *this* cannot be con-sidered." "You can share with me, but it has to come with this filter." "I'm glad to hear you out, but I only have a few minutes before my next important commitment." "I'm open to all ideas, but I've already come to some conclusions."

Asking questions is an excellent way to avoid following through with these kinds of internal decisions, even if you've already had some initial thoughts like this. It is hard to hang on to the belief, "I already have this figured out," while asking good, engaging questions.

WHAT DOES GOOD QUESTIONING SOUND LIKE AND WHAT IS IT NOT?

IT *IS*	IT IS *NOT*
Brief, open-ended, non-leading questions	Close-ended or leading questions, or you speaking the majority of the time
Questions that build on what they say instead of what you had already planned to say when the discussion began	Rapid-fire interrogation rooted in your vision for the conversation
Questions that allow someone to expand their thinking if their current thoughts are narrow *or* to refine their thoughts if they are thinking too broadly	Questions or statements that allow for little exploration. This might include providing opinions too readily or taking their first answer as their only answer.
Using simple prompts like, "What else?" or "Could you share more about that?" or "What other thoughts does that inspire?"	Asking elaborate or lengthy questions that could be confusing or misdirecting

ASKING GOOD QUESTIONS

Let's put this into practice! We'll choose the question at each juncture in Xiao and Jeri's story and see where it takes us.

Xiao calls his manager, Jeri, about an upcoming client meeting.

"Jeri, do you have a minute to discuss the Southeast Financial project? I have an upcoming meeting, and I'd value your perspective."

Xiao presents Jeri with her first decision point:

- Make a statement: "Sure, I can help with that! I think a good course of action could be …"
- Ask a question: "Sure, I'd be glad to help! What are your initial thoughts on an approach to the meeting?"

Note that both could be perceived as supportive. If Jeri makes that statement, her intentions are not necessarily wrong. She just wants to help, and she does have some thoughts or perspective. *And* is that the *best* way to support, develop, and demonstrate respect for Xiao?

She chooses a question.

"Sure, I'd be glad to help! What are your initial thoughts on an approach to the meeting?"

"Well, I know that price is going to be really important to them. In the end, that does drive a lot of their decisions. But I know our plan is good, and I'm confident that it's really what they need. It's the right solution to their needs. I think I'd be shooting myself in the foot if I swept their price concerns under the rug, but I want to redirect them to the problem and how what I'm offering can fit great into providing a solution."

Xiao provides a good overall strategy and another fork in the road where Jeri has a decision — make a statement or ask a question.

- Make a statement: "That's a great perspective, and it's clear you've really thought this through. I was thinking that if we started with the problem, we could simply address price on the back end of the discussion. That way, we don't ignore price, and it's not the focal point of the conversation."
- Ask a question: "That's a great perspective, and it's clear you've really thought this through. What's your sense of how the client would prefer us to approach it?"

Jeri knows Xiao is capable and likely has some intuition in this situation based on his experience. She asks another question.

"That's a great perspective, and it's clear you have really thought this through. What's your sense of how the client would prefer us to approach it?"

"Well, that's what I've really been wrestling with. I think I have to plan to discuss price proactively, or I'd risk them thinking I wasn't listening to them. I wonder if there's an opportunity to recognize that price is part of the conversation right up front but guide them into a discussion about my proposal first. And then, we could approach the price once I've gauged their engagement in the discussion of the solution. What do you think?"

Now, Xiao is asking Jeri directly for her opinion. Surely, she has a green light to share her opinion now, right?

- Make a statement: "That's fantastic logic, and I largely agree. I'd suggest you phrase the pricing upfront by leading with …"
- Ask a question: "That's fantastic logic, and it makes sense to me. What types of risks and benefits could be in play if you tried this tactic?"

Jeri has growing data to suggest that Xiao is in a position to figure this out on his own. She reminds herself that this is about him and his self-discovery and learning. Jeri is articulating support and engagement. At the same time, she trusts that her team member already has many of the right answers, particularly if she can help him process his thoughts.

"That's fantastic logic, and it makes sense to me. What types of risks and benefits could be in play if you tried this tactic?" she asks enthusiastically.

He thinks for a moment and responds, "I think the risk is that they expect it to be addressed fully up front, but I think I can avoid that by simply assuring them that we'll get to that. I think I've built enough rapport for them to trust me to guide the conversation. The benefit seems to be clear — we could spend the bulk of the time collaborating on solutions to their concerns and our role in that. This will give me the space to get into a lot of depth about the time and pain we would be saving them. By the time we get to the prices, there's a great chance they won't be as focused on the price tag!"

Jeri has yet to offer advice at this point. So, what does she do next?

- Make a statement: "I think those benefits point to this being the right approach. Well done! I'd like to support you by ..."
- Ask a question: "It sounds like you're making a pretty good case for this approach. Well done! If that's your plan, how did you see me supporting you best?"

In a conversation with a contributor like Xiao, Jeri might never make a statement and still convey full support for him. For example, he may respond to this last question with something like, "I don't think I need anything right now, but this conversation has been really helpful." In that case, Jeri has provided exactly what Xiao needed from her.

I've seen this result in countless conversations, both in my formal people leadership positions and also in my executive coaching. In fact, I've had occasions where a client has talked for a while and then apologized for talking too much or going on for too long. I assure or remind them that our sessions are built exactly that way. If I'm talking for any more than five minutes in an hour session and that doesn't consist primarily of questions, I am not serving my client well. To take it one step further, a significant benefit of this type of coaching is to simply allow space for the client to "think out loud."

You might be saying, "Yeah, that's a great story with Xiao, Matt, but some folks just don't have good ideas!"

Or some might argue, "All of that question-asking sounds great, but sometimes my people just need me to give them the answer. After all, what is my experience worth if not for helping in that way?"

And to those who take that stance, I say — you're right! You're right. Some people have dumb ideas that need to be corrected. Some team members have never walked that road (you'll learn more in Chapter 5 about my building analogy) and are relying on you and your expertise. Sometimes, our team members are coming to us for answers they *don't* have.

And *nothing* in this exchange has limited Jeri's ability to be that expert advisor to Xiao at any stage of the conversation.

For example, what if she had asked one of her insightful questions, and Xiao responded that he didn't know? What if he had shared an idea that would risk their business with this client? What if they just came to the end of Xiao's knowledge, and he threw up his hands as if to suggest, "Well, I just don't know, Jeri!"

She could offer ideas. She could course correct. She could offer all the answers. In a worst-case scenario, she could even punish or criticize if what Xiao shared was inappropriate.

The key is that great leaders recognize that most of their people have many of the answers they need. A leader's *primary* role is to help the individual find their own answers. Their secondary purpose, and the lever they can pull at any point in the process, is to mentor, teach, or train.

 **COACHING HABIT #1 – FOCUSING ON OTHERS**

HABIT IS SEEN AS: CURIOUS AND CARING
VALUE OR BELIEF BEHIND THIS HABIT: IT'S ABOUT THEM

BEING DIFFERENT FOR DIFFERENT PEOPLE

Have you ever considered how you show up differently for different people? What is your obligation as a leader or potential leader — either formally or informally — to adjust your behaviors, your process, and your level of attention to detail based on the person you're interacting with?

How willing are you to make those adjustments? How many of these adjustments *should* be your responsibility? (I know, "should" is a dangerous word! More on that later in Chapter 5 about Coaching Habit #3 – Being Intentionally Proactive.)

I'm convinced that good leadership is *always* about being what others need you to be. Current conventional wisdom suggests that this need is only growing. More and more employees are expecting or even demanding their leaders to "meet them where they are." This quote from Scott from my survey describes well how being kind is simply not enough:

> *"My first corporate manager was very kind but disinterested. We had zero conversations about development and how I could stretch myself to contribute more. In hindsight, I now see that she was stuck in her own journey. That role quickly became stagnant, and many in the company became apathetic regarding the company's growth."*

WHY IS THIS SO IMPORTANT?

So, first, what is your motivation? What is the "why" behind you exerting all the effort it takes to adjust your own behavior to be different for different people?

Here are three reasons why adjusting your behavior is the most effective way to build trust and rapport with the people you lead:

1. *Demonstrating respect:*

When you approach people in the manner they prefer to interact, you are implicitly saying, "My relationship with you is valuable enough to me that:

- I learned how you'd prefer to work, and
- I'm willing to demonstrate some/many of those behaviors when I interact with you — even if they're not typical for me."

2. *Advancing to solutions more quickly:*

If you are providing the support, information, and/or communication in a way that's most palatable for the recipient, you inherently move closer to solutions or next steps. For example, let's say someone you're working with prefers to have lots of information. You *could* spend time and energy trying to convince them that they don't need that much information in order to do what you're asking of them. Alternatively, if you approached this same person by giving them some portion of the information you think they need in order to feel comfortable to proceed, you're equipping them to take an action or deliver an opinion more quickly. You meet your needs or get closer to them while respecting the other's preferred way to operate.

3. *Demonstrating some understanding of good personal interaction:*

"I live by the 'be easy to' mantra. Be easy to ... work with, do business with, talk to, connect with ... just 'be easy to.'"
— **Jill Schnarr,** quoted in Dan Pontefract's book *The Purpose Effect*

When you meet people where they are, you are being easy to interact with. You're essentially saying, "I can't guarantee what we're about to do will succeed, but I can commit to being a part of the solution as opposed to part of the problem."

> **I can't guarantee what we're about to do will succeed, but I can commit to being a part of the solution as opposed to part of the problem.**

The most common concerns I hear about this type of approach are, "Wouldn't I be sacrificing my authenticity? Won't this make me a phony?" and, "Why should I have to sacrifice who I am in order to interact with others?" (These challenges also come up when discussing how to implement learning gained from personality assessments.)

I have two responses to these legitimate concerns:

1. When exploring the "why" of this tactic, I described a leader who is respectful, easy to work with, efficient, and effective. How closely does that align with how *you* would like to show up to others? It's likely that you'd value those attributes in others, as well as the ability to show up that way yourself.

   a. If you looked at this concern through this lens, how possible is it that adjusting your behaviors to meet someone else's need is *more* about you being authentic to your core values as opposed to distancing yourself from them?

2. We have all those personality attributes in us — our brand of being results-oriented or people-oriented, for example. We are simply dialing up our version of those behaviors for mutual benefit.

   a. Even if the trait or behavior is an area of opportunity for us, it is rarely completely absent in us. We are just being intentional about drawing as much of what we have out of us.

Focusing on others allows us to create common ground, build trust, signal respect for the other person, and advance our own goals more effectively and efficiently.

So, how do we identify what others need of us? Coaching Habit #2 helps us tackle that question.

CHAPTER 4

COACHING HABIT #2
RECOGNIZING WHAT'S NEEDED OF YOU

Habit Is Seen As: Humbly Confident
Value or Belief Behind This Habit: You Meet Them Where They Are

We've established some ways adjusting your behavior might lead to better relationships with your team members — the "why" behind its importance.

With this next coaching habit, it will now be possible to construct the "how" of these interactions.

We'll start by assessing what's needed. Chapter 3 gave some good guidance on how to ask questions. Let's put that to work!

SETTING THE STAGE

Before we discuss how assessments might be applied to your development and your interactions with others, we'll hear from Rachel Pritz, a friend and colleague who is also an expert in one of these assessments: the Enneagram. She makes the business, skill, and emotional claim on the importance of using assessments, including Enneagram. Rachel shares:

> *Rarely do you see skills like compassionate, self-aware, or emotionally intelligent show up on a resume. These are often called "soft skills," but there's nothing soft about them. It takes daily intention and effort to learn these skills. It's a journey, not a destination. No book, podcast, or personality assessment will be a quick solution to building these skills. But the Enneagram personality framework can give you a starting point along with a GPS map for your journey.*
>
> *The Enneagram is a personality typing system that describes 9 different types of ways we view the world. Psychologically, we created these patterns of behavior in childhood. They were meant to protect us, but as we carry these into adulthood, they can often be limitations. The Enneagram wakes you up to these patterns of behavior and helps you uncover what motivates you to behave a certain way in the first place. It shows you the good, the bad, and the ugly. It's all about dismantling the ego (aka personality) and coming out the other side with more self-wisdom and understanding of the people around us. Learning the shadow sides of ourselves can be hurtful and even downright embarrassing. But we can't make*

real change and grow into our full potential without being willing to get uncomfortable.

Here are 5 key areas of growth that the Enneagram can unlock in you.

1. **Find your motivator**

   We often know our behavior is less than desirable, but it's rare that we take the time to understand why that behavior came out in the first place. Each of the 9 types has a specific core motivation or why. Knowing this can help us recognize when our ego is in the driver's seat. It can also help us understand our triggers, which can ultimately change poor behaviors.

2. **Clarity on stress and growth**

   The advantage of the Enneagram is that it's dynamic. It doesn't put someone in a box with a number. In fact, it says here's your box, but let's take the lid off, tear down the sides and let you run. Each one of the types has specific stress and growth arrows. This means when we are stressed or growing, the behaviors of another personality type (or number) come out. This can explain why we look and even feel so different in periods of stress and growth. Why is this important? When you start to see stress behaviors, call a timeout. Ask yourself how you got there. What needs to happen to get you out? When you see areas of growth, reflect on how you got there. Rinse and repeat.

3. **Validates you**

   Good news! Nothing is wrong with you. Finding out many other people show up in the world in a similar way can be liberating. I can't tell you the number of clients that start sentences with, "you are going to think I'm crazy ......" My usual response is that I don't think they are crazy at all because 3 other people of their same type just told me the same thing this week.

4. ***Depersonalizes other people's behavior***
When we learn about all the Enneagram types, it helps us find grace and compassion for the unique ways we all show up. We all have core fears, core desires, and core motivations. When someone directs their poor behavior toward you, it rarely has anything to do with you. Metaphorically, just pat them on the head, say aww.... You haven't done your work on this yet, and I'm not going to make that mean anything more than it does.

5. ***Precision leadership***
Understanding the way your team sees the world can build relationships with the team you lead. The golden rule is "treat people the way you want to be treated." The platinum rule is "treat people the way they want to be treated." That's a whole new level of leadership.[2]

UNPACKING PERSONALITY ASSESSMENTS

Full disclosure: I am a big fan of assessments and have invested a lot of time into learning about several different types: personality, motivational, behavioral, and attitudinal.

I am licensed in many tools and have been exposed through reading or experience to many more. (I invite you to visit my website at *mattdickersonvalued.com* for a quick reference guide to common personality assessments.)

I find assessments to be the quickest way to access knowledge about personality types and preferences. We can also use this knowledge for the benefit of social interaction and personal leadership.

The power in these tools is the self-discovery that is possible, which then becomes functional when two people can discuss the results using the common language of that particular assessment tool.

I work daily to be more knowledgeable in this space. From my deep dive into the assessment world, I have drawn some initial conclusions:

- No one assessment is superior to others.
  - Multiple assessments claim 80-90 percent validity based on various metrics.
  - Fundamentally, these assessments serve as vehicles for self-discovery. Focusing on which tool is better or best can take away from focusing on the person participating in the exercise. The participant's perception of value from the exercise is the primary objective, and anything that diminishes or gets in the way of that discovery is problematic.
  - I have personally witnessed transformative results from almost a dozen different types of assessments. Similarly, I have witnessed many of those same assessments that were successful for one client to fall flat with another. The determining factor between

an assessment encounter being helpful or productive or not is more dependent on the engagement of the participant, not the tool used.

- Assessments are not likely to accurately assess future performance or evaluate fit for a particular position/role.
  - What many assessments *can* effectively do is shed light on some of our natural tendencies or personality traits. Examples of such tools include DiSC, Insights Discovery, Core Values Index, and 5 Voices. These tools also give us insight into how the people we interact with might be predisposed to certain needs, fears, desires, or preferred ways of working.
  - What they *don't* do is predict the person's ability to fulfill the duties of a job — nor can they anticipate someone's personal satisfaction in doing so.[3]

FINDING A LEADERSHIP VOICE

Sara walked into the large conference room of the hotel. She did it with no great urgency because she really didn't want to be there.

"I'm probably going to be asked about my feelings," she sighed to herself. "If I have to share too much today, I might just quit," she mumbled, only half-joking.

Her mind was spinning.

"I didn't even want this stupid job in the first place," she lamented. "I was doing just fine working in my own little world. And then they asked me to lead a team!" To say she was trapped in a negative head space would be an understatement.

"I was getting great reviews, producing well, and enjoying my job because I felt like my talents were really being used. Now I'm trapped in this manager role, babysitting adults and pushing paper!

"Worse yet, I have to come to things like this and talk about my feelings!"

Sara sat down at the only empty table she found, despite knowing most of the twenty-five people at this Insights Discovery workshop. They worked in the same department but in different roles and responsibilities. Their leader believed participation in this workshop about personality types would help them interpersonally.

Participants had been asked to complete a questionnaire, and the facilitators had reviewed these ahead of time. The majority of the group did not self-assess as "people people." Due to the nature of their work (research), it made sense that they would largely be a group of detail- and task-oriented people who would value process and procedure.

Sara had just been promoted to manager of her team, where she'd been a star individual contributor. When a leadership position opened, she was quickly inserted despite having no formal manager training. She'd never expressed an interest to lead but was hesitant to decline the offer.

She listened politely as the facilitators gave some background on the assessment and an overall education on the tool and the philosophy.

Thirty minutes in, Sara was feeling some relief. "So far, so good," she thought to herself. "I just have to sit here and listen to this for another three hours and thirty minutes, and then I can make my escape!"

But her luck was short-lived. Soon, they began to pass out each person's report, and it was time for self-discovery!

"Why do I even need to go through this? I know who I am. What good is this going to bring me?" Sara was struggling to dive into the data.

Then she started to see statements in the report that rang true. Not all the descriptions fit her, but many of them did. And reading some of them, she thought, "How in the world could a test like this know that about me?!"

"Okay, this is mildly interesting, but I still don't see how it could be helpful," she thought.

As the facilitator brought them back together from their individual review, he asked, "How was that experience?" Several people raised their hands, and a few shared.

And then he said, "I bet at least some of you are thinking, 'Well, this is great, but I don't see how this helps me in my day-to-day life. What's the point of this?'"

Sara flinched. "Are they reading my mind now, too?"

The facilitator continued. "If that's the case, you're asking the right questions, and this next part is for you!"

"By asking yourself just a couple of questions, you might be able to take an educated guess about someone else's personality type." He put a slide with these questions up on the screen:

- Is this person more methodical in their work, or do they like to act or decide more quickly? Would you consider them more extroverted and outspoken or introverted and more thoughtful?
  - Methodical, Introverted, Thoughtful – Blue or Green
  - Quick-Acting, Extroverted, Outspoken – Red or Yellow

- Is this person more focused on people or on details and tasks? Do they prefer to work collaboratively with other people, or do they excel at individual work?
  - Focused on People, Work Collaboratively – Yellow or Green
  - Focused on Details and Tasks, Excels at (prefers) Individual Work – Blue or Red

He went on, "Think of a coworker you work closely with; maybe one you struggle to get along with." There were a few chuckles from the room. Sara could think of several!

The facilitator guided them, "Are they outgoing and fast-paced, or more methodical and tend to keep to themselves?"

"Definitely fast-paced," she answered to herself. The guy she was thinking of never stopped!

"Okay, we have the first half of the puzzle! Now, are they more concerned with people or tasks? Do they value conversations or data?"

"Oh boy," she thought, "this guy was all about the people. All he wanted to do was *chat!*"

"Now," the leader implored, "think back to the last time you felt a disconnect with them. Was it a meeting or a phone call? Was it an email? Was it during a presentation?"

It was a video conference call. Sara remembered it clearly. Ted is one of her more "enthusiastic" direct reports. He was particularly amped up during last week's team meeting, which was a little weird because the group is going through a lot of change. Let's just say there's not a lot to be excited about.

The facilitator put a new set of questions up on the screen and encouraged the group to spend some time reflecting and jotting down some notes.

- Based on your basic diagnosis of their personality you just conducted, how do you think that influences how they viewed that interaction? With what bias would you guess they came to that encounter? Based *just* on their personality, what do you think they hoped to get out of that email/meeting/discussion? How did they want to *feel* as a result of it? How do you think they *did* feel?

Sara carefully read the questions and began to process. Her thought process went something like this:

> "Well, I have a better understanding that I'm not naturally going to be the upbeat and fun member of the group. Not that that's bad; it's just my tendency, my preference. So, when Ted shows up like that, it's already different from what my normal reaction would be and, therefore, a little surprising. I'm starting with a disconnection just based on prefer- ence. When you think about it, it's not really Ted's fault that he's naturally enthusiastic — just like it's not my fault that I value steadi- ness, process, and predictability. It's just what we like."

She thought about it more.

> "It's true that we're going through a lot of change. I'm looking for resolve in my team. I need to know I can count on them through

all of this. What is Ted thinking? What does he need?

"Well, I bet he's looking for something in this change, too. It's broken to him, too, just probably in a different way. If this personality stuff has any truth to it, he's probably trying to keep our mood positive because that's important to him. He might be worried about losing the fun through all the swirling change."

You can see what Sara is processing at this moment. She better understands herself and how her predisposition can assign truths about a situation, such as, "We shouldn't be so jovial during such uncertain times." That is not as much a truth as it is her opinion — based on her personality style and perception. This is also a peek into who Ted is and what he might value. Ted is potentially showing up in the way that (1) best aligns with his personality and (2) is likely the way he thinks he should be for the team.

Sara is making her learning actionable. She can now adjust her thoughts and her actions based on this simple yet important information.

BUT WHAT IF YOU CAN'T TAKE A COURSE?

Showing up differently for different people might include becoming knowledgeable in one of these disciplines. Maybe it starts with you experiencing one of these tools.

Perhaps your company is set up to offer a team assessment. Or maybe you could pursue this type of experience through an outside vendor.

Many of these assessments have books, articles, and resources that are easily available without taking a course. Ideally, you'd have an experience facilitated by a trained professional with the ability to unpack your interpretations with a trained coach. But in the absence of that option, you could quickly develop a basic understanding of the concepts.

USING DiSC PERSONALITY ASSESSMENT AS AN EXAMPLE

Let's look at this through the lens of the personality assessment DiSC, in part because it is one of the more commonly used.

The four letters in DiSC represent four personality traits: dominance, influence, steadiness, and conscientiousness. You may find different words applied to these four letters, depending on where you're reading. In his original writings, William Moulton Marston defined them as dominance, inducement, submission, and compliance. These words have been updated in various ways to adapt to more common language in present times, but the structure and definitions remain aligned with his original theories.

For the sake of our example, let's assume you have a meeting coming up with someone who's not unlike Ted from our previous example. You've observed that they're outgoing and personable, and they like to have fun.

They're focused on moving projects forward with some urgency but are also very conscious about people in the process. They also have lots of ideas. By reviewing a PDF you've downloaded from the internet that gives basic descriptions of personality types in DiSC, you can quickly make an educated guess that this person leads with a lot of *influence* (i).

With that knowledge, you can approach them slightly differently in your next meeting.

For example, you can plan to build some small talk into your conversation. Someone with these personality traits is more likely to want to hear about your weekend (or, more probably, tell you about theirs!).

You know they're less likely to be interested in hearing a bunch of details and more prone to presenting several of their own ideas. Knowing that, you could prepare to be more inviting of their ideas. You might also plan ways to encourage them to narrow their next steps in order to act on these ideas in a manageable way.

You'll notice that I'm using terms like more or less probable or likely. That is intentional. Even if you were highly educated in this type of personality assessment and used it with success in the past, each person is unique. They have different experiences, different opinions, varied seasons of life, and dozens of other things about them that mean you'll only ever be guessing. You haven't cracked the code of humankind or even this individual. What you are doing is taking a step toward a greater probability of connection. You're decreasing the chance of obstacles and increasing the probability of a successful conversation.

COACHING HABIT #2 – RECOGNIZING WHAT'S NEEDED OF YOU

HABIT IS SEEN AS: HUMBLY CONFIDENT
VALUE OR BELIEF BEHIND THIS HABIT: YOU MEET THEM WHERE THEY ARE

A NEW LEARNING WORKSHOP EXPERIENCE... FOR THE FACILITATOR

A couple of years ago, I led an Insights Discovery workshop with my team of ten and a few of my peers. As I shared earlier in this chapter, I am a big fan of using personality assessments for self-discovery, and this is one of many I've come to understand better.

Similar to DiSC, Insights details four "color energies" that we all have in some ratio. If you're high in one color, you are said to be leading with that color energy. No energy is better than another, and being low in one does not mean that you *can't* lead with that type of personality. It might mean that you expend more energy doing it because it's not the type of activity or interaction that you're drawn to.

I took the team through some basic understanding of the history and philosophy of the tool. Next, we dug into their self-assessments, and I helped them digest what this information could mean to them. They were really absorbing the content, and the experience was going great!

Then I did something I don't normally do when leading a workshop like this. I realized this situation was unique because they each knew me well. In that moment, I became very curious about how *they* viewed *me*.

I asked them, "Now that you have a bit of understanding of the color energies, with what energy do you think I lead? Jot down that color on a Post-it note and bring it up to me." They gave it some thought and came to relatively quick decisions.

What happened next was one of the greatest compliments I have ever received professionally, even if it took me several weeks to fully unpack its significance.

As I turned over the notes, one by one, something funny happened. Remember, they were guessing what color energy I led with the most. I turned the first one over: Yellow. Yellow energy is outgoing and results-oriented. It is collaborative and people-oriented, as well, but for the purpose of achieving things. This is one of my more prominent colors.

I turned over the second note: Blue. This was a little surprising because it is usually the least present color for me. Blue is the color of detail, information, and order. When you lead with blue, you're focused on process and doing things precisely. In other words, *nothing* like me!

I turned the third note over: Yellow. "Okay," I thought, "now we're back on track."

Next: Green. Green is the color energy of the empathetic and caring. This personality is patient and relational. Leading with this energy is something I certainly strive toward, but I could not yet identify it as a lead energy for me.

Then: Red. If someone leads with a lot of red energy, they might be described as action-oriented, extroverted, and driven. On good days, they stay focused on getting things done. In times of stress or anxiety, they may be accused of being overbearing or a "bull in a china shop."

Yellow. Red. Red. Blue. Red. Yellow. And so it went. In other words, their guesses were all over the place.

I said, "That's interesting. Lots of different answers here!"

One of my team members, Scott, spoke up with wisdom that was eluding me at that moment. He shared that he was surprised to find that he was the only person in the room who identified me as leading with green. He admitted to me later that his initial thought was that he'd made a mistake in some way. Perhaps he misunderstood the content. Maybe he had misjudged me. And then it came to him.

He said, "I wonder if you act differently with different people. I wonder if you take on the energy your team member prefers in order to 'meet them where they are.' You're always using that saying!"

Scott continued, "As Matt predicted before this workshop, I lead with a lot of green. And I wrote down green for him."

He's people-oriented and highly reflective. He's one of the deepest thinkers I've worked with, and he exhibits high emotional intelligence. He guessed that I led with a lot of green because that is how he sees me show up in our one-with-one time.

Then another team member offered, "That makes sense because I lead with more red, and I guessed that you led with red. It seems like you're always moving fast and quick to come to a conclusion, and that's part of what I appreciate about you."

As I digested this later, I realized I had moved much closer to the inclusive leader that I was aiming to be (and there's still a lot of work to do). I was adjusting my behavior slightly for each team member with the objective of working together more effectively.

> **I was adjusting my behavior slightly for each team member with the objective of working together more effectively.**

This experience provided some affirmation that I was a very different (and better) version of a leader than I had been.

One team member took me aside as we went to break. She said, "I've heard you use the term 'humbly confident' before. I wonder if the kind of work we are doing with Insights allows us to show up as both humble and confident." I absolutely agree.

 ## COACHING HABIT #2 – RECOGNIZING WHAT'S NEEDED OF YOU

HABIT IS SEEN AS: HUMBLY CONFIDENT
VALUE OR BELIEF BEHIND THIS HABIT: YOU MEET THEM WHERE THEY ARE

Empathy, for example, is both genetic (some people have more of it than others do) and teachable (everyone can learn to have more). But perhaps the greatest discovery is that empathy is the root of two of the most important human activities: It powers our morality, and it drives progress.

— **Jenn Granneman and Andre Sólo**, *Sensitive*

WHAT HAVE YOU CHANGED YOUR MIND ABOUT?

As demonstrated in the example of Sara and Ted, the belief behind this coaching habit is that leaders need to meet those they lead "where they are."

I've learned this lesson over and over as a leader, seeing both the pitfalls of not doing this and the success from its application.

Anyone who's been involved in my professional development knows that my growth has been riddled with missteps and about-faces in my understanding of self, my approach to working with others, and my philosophies toward investing in others.

One of my favorite podcasts is Dave Stachowiak's *Coaching for Leaders*. As of the writing of this book, Dave has recorded over 640 episodes of his podcast. He has interviewed anyone who is anyone in professional development, leadership, and contemporary thinking in business.

It's common for him to end interviews by asking his guest, "What have you recently changed your mind about?" The brilliance of this question is only exceeded by the amazing answers it produces.

I'm proud to report that I've changed my mind a lot when it comes to what good leadership is. And in the process, I've learned much about myself. This also provides an important example of why personality assessments can't fully predict future outcomes.

One of my great journeys was facilitated rapidly by coach training. I learned *how* to listen better. I also learned that listening, while not always natural, was the tool by which I would best achieve my ultimate professional goal: feed into the growth of others as often and effectively as possible. In other words, I couldn't be good at what I felt called to do without employing this skill frequently and consistently.

ASSESSMENTS CAN BE INSIGHTFUL, BUT NOT NECESSARILY PREDICTIVE

My evolution provides a reasonable example of the *predictive* value of most assessments. In all assessments I've participated in, my natural inclination to talk more than I listen is confirmed. However, I've learned that listening more than talking is how I achieve my goals for myself professionally. Therefore, I am continuously motivated to act outside of my natural tendencies in order to meet those goals. The benefit greatly exceeds the cost for me.

Insights Discovery, as featured in Sara's story earlier in the chapter, is one of several personality profiles that has its roots in the work of Carl Jung and also follows a much-used quadrant model of categorizing personality profiles. Let's use it to explore this idea more deeply.

Jungian theory proposes that each individual has a conscious and a less conscious persona. At its most basic, the less conscious is who we are when no one is watching and we are relying most minimally on "outside forces" — who we think we *should* be, what others would think of what we're doing, etc. The conscious persona is how we show up for others. This could change based on several factors, including social norms, our roles and responsibilities, or our perceptions of what we think others want from us.

In this model, Jung suggests that we are commonly capable of exhibiting traits and characteristics of other personality types (or "color energies" in Insights terminology) but that it can come at a cost. There is an energy transfer that occurs when we pursue behaviors that are not our natural tendency. We expend energy if we try to be significantly more or less of a trait than is our preference. In other words, being someone else can be exhausting!

In my coaching, if I notice an apparent energy transfer is occurring — a significant spike or drop in a particular color from less conscious to more conscious — I often ask these questions, in this order:

- Is this accurate based on your reflection or perspective? Is it right?
- Is this needed for your position or responsibilities? Does your role/job require this kind of spike or drop in order to be successful?
- If yes to the first two questions, what do you do to intentionally rejuvenate or recover? Additionally, I might ask, is this what you want? This assumes that Jung is right and that energy has to be expended to make this happen. If energy is lost, how does one recuperate?[4]

In my case, it takes me a lot more energy to focus on others in conversation. I must be intentional about suppressing my self-interest and my desire to share — to talk. If someone were to predict my ability or my willingness to serve as a supportive coach or an empathetic leader based on my personality assessment scores, they might be right to predict that

I would struggle or that the role would not be sustainable. These types of assessments routinely suggest that I expend significant energy amping up my others-focused empathy.

However, because coaching and developing others is so aligned with my core values, and I gain so much personal satisfaction from it, it is often naturally rejuvenating for me. Its purpose in the lives of those I seek to serve, and subsequently the purpose in my life, is enough to make this "stretch" practice of mine viable long-term.

In this way, I defy any perception of predictability about future outcomes that could be derived from personality assessments.

CHAPTER 5

COACHING HABIT #3
BEING INTENTIONALLY PROACTIVE

Habit Is Seen As: Advocate for Growth
Value or Belief Behind this Habit: You Facilitate Their Growth

> For me, the language 'I decide' is very powerful, whether it's deciding how I show up or deciding what my next step in something is. This doesn't ensure a particular outcome or necessarily impact those around me, but it does provide a sense of grounding and choice about how I respond to my internal and external environment, no matter what my surroundings hold.
> — **Kelsy Trigg**, quoted in Dan Pontefract, *The Purpose Effect*

This quote from *The Purpose Effect* is so powerful, in part because it focuses on "I decide." Pontefract goes on to say the decision points occur in both how I show up and in what my next step in something is.

Let's spend a moment with each.

I DECIDE...HOW I SHOW UP

From the Stoics of the late BC period and the early AD period to modern-day philosophers and assessment gurus, much thought has gone into what we control. Or, in this terminology, what we "decide."

Much of this has to do with our internal narrative — what we tell ourselves, often repetitively. We'll explore internal and external narratives and go into great detail on how they interact in Chapter 8 (Coaching Habit #6 – Driving Results).

For now, we will wrestle with the idea that *you* have control over how *you* show up in any given situation.

As you've read the first few chapters of this book and come to a better understanding of your role in the development of others, you've likely already begun to think about how you can be an active participant in this role.

Yet, to have that impact or embark on that journey, you need to *decide* to enter that arena.

As this decision point relates to developing others, I am reminded of an interaction I had with one of my direct reports — let's call him Martin.

Martin had been a member of our team for about nine months and was doing well in the role. He'd excelled in training and had made an impact in his sales territory in a short amount of time.

He was already executing at a level that allowed us to have more advanced development conversations. For example, I was considering which contacts I could introduce him to from other departments or elsewhere.

One day, Martin messed up. We were conducting an in-person sales call together, and he asked for a decision-maker with whom it was difficult to meet. In fact, this customer was normally closed off from us, and we did not have a great relationship.

As we waited in the lobby for the contact to be retrieved, Martin received a phone call. He answered the phone call and stepped around the corner to speak. During this time, the contact could have come out, or those trying to find the contact could have returned with an update or request. In that case, Martin would not have been available to interact with them.

His phone call concluded, and soon thereafter, one of the staff returned to say our contact was unavailable, but he would welcome our call at a later time.

As we walked out of the customer's office, I asked some open-ended questions about his impression of the call.

"I'm a little disappointed we weren't able to speak with X, but I feel like we have some good follow-up opportunities, and I did everything I could to meet with the right people." He spoke casually and also with a bit of confidence.

I was surprised. I'd expected him to say something along the lines of, "I probably shouldn't have answered that call, but it was really important for this reason." Instead, he didn't identify taking a phone call as an issue at all. To my further dismay, he later confirmed that he had an inkling the call wasn't that important.

I said, "Frankly, I'm surprised that you would risk upsetting a hard-to-see customer by taking a phone call in their place of business."

I went on to give some tough coaching about his level of professionalism at that moment and share some concern that this might not be a one-off situation.

Initially, he seemed concerned about my assessment, but to his credit, he showed up as very coachable, and that resulted in a productive conversation.

We stopped for some lunch, and after retrieving our food, I said, "So, I wanted to follow up on our development conversation." We'd planned this discussion earlier. He was quiet.

I offered, "I think the best next step for you is to expand your internal network, and I have a couple of ideas as to how you might go about that in the coming weeks."

His face reflected a mixture of confusion and appreciation.

He kind of snorted as if he was trying to comprehend the incomprehensible. "Wait, you want to talk about career development after my screw-up in that last office?"

I responded with measured enthusiasm. "Definitely! We'd planned to discuss next steps during our time together today. Nothing that happened on that last sales call prohibits us from doing that."

"But you and I both know I really messed up on that last call. Doesn't that put some doubt in your mind that I'm ready for any kind of next steps?"

I set down my sandwich and said flatly, "No."

I continued, "You are excelling in your position, and you're capable of so much beyond this role. A prerequisite for these conversations is not perfection. You still have a lot to learn in your current role, but that doesn't mean we can't keep your development outside of your role going."

As his leader and the person who was tasked with holding him accountable for not meeting expectations, I had every right to table any development conversation. Delaying those next steps for a future time, in light of his infraction, would have been appropriate.

However, I *decided* that I was going to follow appropriate tough coaching with developmental tactics.

I *decided* that he'd not done something so terrible that it negated his work from the previous months.

I *decided* that his development would remain a primary topic for our time together and that we'd decide on what he could do next to advance his skill set and his internal brand in the organization.

I *decided* that his development was more important than holding a one-off action against him.

> **I *decided* that his development was more important than holding a one-off action against him.**

The second aspect of the Pontefract quote is:

I DECIDE . . . WHAT MY NEXT STEP IN SOMETHING IS

None of us needs to have it all figured out. No one has to fully understand or correctly predict what they will be doing in ten years or five years or even two years.

This doesn't mean we shouldn't have a vision for ourselves or for those we might informally or formally lead.

What we should focus on, though, is our next steps in front of where we are now.

Have you ever had a situation so big, or so complex, or so confusing, or so overwhelming that you felt stuck? Have you been in a situation where the outcome seems so far off you simply can't fathom where things will take you?

It's often helpful to think about the task in front of you as a series of next steps.

- What do I need to do today?
- What needs to be accomplished before anything else can be decided?
- What is most urgent in the timeline?
- Who is the next person I need to engage?

Answers to these questions allow us some direction in a directionless situation. As those steps unfold, new information frequently becomes available, or new solutions are presented. We can then use the same questions as a filter for discovering subsequent steps.

Just as you would encourage someone you're coaching or mentoring to find these next steps, you can also apply this same tactic to your support of their development. It is *your* decision as to how proactively you want to invest in their growth.

COACHING HABIT #3 – BEING INTENTIONALLY PROACTIVE

HABIT IS SEEN AS: ADVOCATE FOR GROWTH
VALUE OR BELIEF BEHIND THIS HABIT: YOU FACILITATE THEIR GROWTH

One thing he's learned from his studies is that culture and traditions affect the quality of loneliness and connectedness by shaping our social expectations. Loneliness, Ami told me, occurs when our social experience fails to meet our social expectations. We tend to feel lonely when something goes 'wrong,' and we don't make friends the way we 'should' or marry the person we 'should' or interact with our neighbors and colleagues as we 'should.' All these 'shoulds' quietly seep into us as we grow up.
— **Dr. Ami Rokach,** quoted in Vivek Murthy, *Together*

The feelings of powerlessness that often accompany failure start with those all-too-familiar 'could have' or 'should have' self-inventories. And our fear grows in tandem with the strength of our belief that an opening has been forever closed.
— **Brené Brown,** *Rising Strong*

WHO SHOULD DRIVE (SCHEDULE, INITIATE, GUIDE) DEVELOPMENT CONVERSATIONS?

Depending on the organization, the leaders and the direct reports have sole responsibility or share some responsibility for preparing, scheduling, driving, and capturing outcomes for these interactions.

But whose *should* it be?

As the quote from Dr. Rokach suggests, there is a risk to "should thinking."

As a certified coach, I often find myself steering my clients away from conversations involving *should*. "Should" gets us into trouble. My boss *should* have given me that opportunity. My colleague *should* have been more receptive to my idea. I *should* have gotten the lead on that project. My kids *should* listen to me more — I know what I'm talking about! My company *should* venture into X area. I almost wrote a book called *Death by Should*. (Sounds ominous, right?)

Consider this experiment:

Have you ever noticed that when you get a new car, all of a sudden, you see that exact car everywhere you go? It's doubtful that this particular model or color has multiplied on the streets overnight. It *is* likely that your new car has become, however brief, a focus of your attention.

So, here's the experiment. Take the next couple of days or weeks and keep an ear out for the word "should." When you hear it, pause to ask yourself a few questions:

- In what context is the word being used?
  - Is someone rendering a complaint or a concern?
  - Is it being articulated in "the heat of the moment"?
  - Is the speaker referring to themselves or someone or something else?
- In what ways would the comment have a different meaning or connotation if the word "should" was absent? What if they said "could" instead? What if that whole part of the comment was removed?

- What do you notice as a result of this reflection? How do those observations impact your view of the situation?

In addition to the benefits of uncovering the word "should" in coaching engagements, the word may also be a red flag for some disconnection or misunderstanding.

However, in this case, let's venture into the perilous world of "should." What *should* our devotion to personal professional development be? What *should* our commitment be to our people? What *should* we owe them when it comes to their development?

BREAK FOR SELF-REFLECTION:

I'd invite you to pause and explore these questions for yourself:

> If you're a new leader, what's your initial impression of who is responsible for development? If you've been leading for a while, how has your opinion changed (or not) over time? What do you think has impacted that change?

There seems to be a popular school of thought that individuals should take accountability for their own development. While I don't disagree with accountability and responsibility, I fear we frequently overestimate an individual's ability and knowledge to chart their own course.

Brittani, a middle manager at a global medical company, shared a common (and not unjust) insight. She put it this way in my survey feedback:

> *"Not all employees have the same drive or passion that I have to develop and grow professionally. It's important to support and guide individuals, but ultimately, they have to want to pursue opportunities."*

Anyone who's worked with me for any period of time has heard my analogy of asking someone to build a house (a collection of former mentees just let out a collective moan).

We often say, "If Andre really wants to develop in his career, he should show initiative/be proactive/come up with ways in which to develop and do them!" If Andre does step up and demonstrate something innovative or stretch in a new direction, he is proving his self-efficacy and, in some way, legitimizes whatever time we want to put into his development. If he doesn't, then the most likely explanation is that he does not have the requisite drive or capabilities to step up to the challenges in front of him.

The problem frequently is that Andre has no idea what his next steps are or how to formulate a plan. And ... that has *nothing* to do with his self-efficacy. It has everything to do with his lack of knowledge about what "next" looks like.

ENTER THE BUILDING ANALOGY!

In this parlance, we deliver Andre the message that if he cares about his career and his self-development, he will go build a house. But Andre says, "I don't know how to build a house. I've never built a house before. I'm not familiar with the process. In fact, I don't even know where to start. I don't know where to get the plans, and I don't know any contractors or people who could advise me."

Sadly, our response as leadership teams (or leaders) in this situation is often, "Andre, if you really care about your career and your development, you will build that house!"

It might seem like a silly analogy, but it seems to land the point I hope to make: if someone has not walked the road, how can they self-direct? How do they know what skills are needed for the next step or how to develop them? How could they be expected to navigate company culture above their pay grade if they have little-to-no experience with those stakeholders? How could they be expected to know the best advisors to pick and how to engage them if they've had no previous contact with them? How do they know what questions to ask or what ideas they should pursue?

How can they build a house if they have no experience in house building?

And let us ask ourselves a tough question: What is it about *us* that leads us to think their development is their own responsibility? I cannot possibly diagnose, but I pose this as a question for some reflection.

"Well, Matt," you might say, "how else are they going to prove themselves — their drive, their competence, their proactivity?"

In my experience, they prove all of that after they've been given some initial direction, instruction, and encouragement. Give them an inch; they take a mile — that's what high-performing, high-potentials do. They accept your guidance and suggestions, and they learn well. They prove themselves after the suggestions, not before.

> **They prove themselves after the suggestions, not before.**

WHEN AND HOW TO HAVE DEVELOPMENT CONVERSATIONS

How Frequently?

This question comes up often. At the risk of sounding hyperbolic, could we ask ourselves a different question? How important a priority is someone's professional development?

Then, based on that response, how often should you chat about it?

Traditionally, development equals performance — another issue in and of itself, but more on that in a moment — and, therefore, should be covered as part of an annual review when an employee receives feedback on their value to the company. Given the expectations of their role, what did they do, and how well did it meet the company's definitions of excellence?

Leadership books are littered with stories of ineptitude in these interactions, such as the absent leader giving erroneous feedback or the clueless leader rendering an ill-informed assessment. Giving bad feedback is part of the problem.

It's also true that giving feedback every twelve months simply does not support personal growth.

But I might argue that an annual review is a symptom of the problem, not the problem itself. If the only evidence of a focus on development is an exercise that doesn't support development, the problem is much more endemic.

Many organizations have instituted some form of mid-year or quarterly reviews that attempt to give the employee and the manager the opportunity to touch base on progress toward performance year-to-date.

There is some debate as to who should drive those conversations — the manager or the employee. One argument goes that the employee should take ownership of the process and demonstrate their self-efficacy by scheduling and leading those conversations.

Personally, I've always felt the onus was on me as the people leader. Whether the discussion surrounded performance or development, I was never too hung up on who initiated it but always felt the weight of that responsibility. If I'm showing up as a good leader, my thinking goes, I owe it to members of my team to guide them whenever I can. I'll speak more about this when we discuss accountability and responsibility for development plans.

I am frequently reminded through my coaching work how important it is to allow people regular opportunities to process verbally, to facilitate depth of discussion. Some people value the ability to be verbal in a safe environment more than others, but generally, it's viewed as a positive attribute of a strong leader, effective mentor, or good teammate.

CREATING SAFE SPACE

I've always been motivated to create an open and safe environment; I haven't always been that great at it. In my worst moments, I am simply the guy who likes to talk a lot. In my better but still misguided moments, I think I must provide information to those without it. My heart wants to give, but I've come to realize that the recipient of my amazing advice usually already knew 90 percent of it and needed none of it.

There are some fundamental ideas that make a space safe for unfiltered sharing:

Set the expectation that you value the conversation and that this is a safe environment.

- Simply making this statement and verbally setting that expectation is a good first step.
- It is up to the leader to prove this safety in the long term. It also requires the leader to restate these assurances "in the heat of the moment."

Give them permission to share openly without having their thoughts fully formed.

- This could be messy. They could say inappropriate things. They could share ideas that are flawed or lack perspective. They could expose elements you've coached or advised them on. They could be critical of you or expose ways in which you have not supported them well. They could say things that offend you or hurt your feelings.

Ask, *"And what else...?"*

- In *The Coaching Habit*, Michael Bungay Stanier calls this the single most compelling question you can ask a person who's clearly wrestling with something.
- According to Stanier, this question does a few critical things, the most important of which is to help you, the coach/leader, self-regulate — shut up and just listen. He also points out that the first thing someone says is rarely the core issue or concern.

GROUND RULES

You're on your way to creating and showing up well for an environment of quality sharing. This also comes with some ground rules:

- You're allowed to have an opinion. Whether it's a mentoring or coaching relationship or even an informal peer-to-peer conversation, you likely know things the other person doesn't. If you can improve their understanding or perspective, it is your obligation to provide it. They've engaged you in this conversation.
  - To mitigate the risk of oversharing on your part, allow them to fully share *first*. Then, ask if your thoughts would be welcome or potentially helpful — ask for permission.
- They do not have the right to demean or abuse you or otherwise violate your core values. Mutual respect is a minimum expectation in a constructive relationship. The

decision may come down to your perception of their motives. If you believe their intent is to clarify their own feelings or thoughts, you may have the opportunity to receive their words with grace. ("They're just venting. I can take it.")

- They don't have complete immunity from all consequences. For example, if someone crosses into sexual harassment, they cannot be saved by invoking the sanctity of the trusting conversation that you promised. Laws and company policies still apply.
- You do not have to ultimately agree with their assessment or conclusions. This is arguably most important in manager/employee scenarios.
  - I've spent most of my career in sales. All salespeople have at least one thing in common: they never agree with the quota they're given. It was common to hear coworkers question the methodology or the reasonableness of the numbers and/or to list the elements of their environment that make these goals unachievable or unfair. It was also common for my direct reports to engage me in conversation about these concerns. Yet it was rare that this resulted in me changing their quotas or any of my own actions.
  - It was, however, important for me to hear their concerns and answer their questions. Frequently, I could provide clarity or perspective that increased their understanding, even if it did not solve their concern. Oftentimes, at the end of these conversations, they'd say something like, "Well, I still don't totally agree, but this conversation has been helpful." If they didn't get there on their own, I might say something like, "I'm glad you brought your concerns to me and that

I could answer some of your questions. At this point, let's discuss plans to meet and exceed these numbers."

So, what else can you do to make these ideas actionable in your day-to-day work? How can you quickly signal to someone you are leading that the environment is collaborative, safe, and focused on benefit to them?

 ## COACHING HABIT #3 – BEING INTENTIONALLY PROACTIVE

HABIT IS SEEN AS: ADVOCATE FOR GROWTH
VALUE OR BELIEF BEHIND THIS HABIT: YOU FACILITATE THEIR GROWTH

Being intentionally proactive is as much about attitude as it is about rigor or process.

I have often told someone I was working with, either as a mentor or, more frequently, as their direct leader, that it's possible that I think about their development more than they do. To be clear, that doesn't mean I'm going to do their development for them. It also does not mean that the person I'm speaking with doesn't prioritize their own development. Finally, it is not meant to be hyperbolic. It is simply the way that I choose to approach investing in people.

As I point out in the Preface and earlier in this chapter, those we coach and lead usually have less visibility of their path or where it leads than we do. If they were proficient in a particular area or they'd developed toward a particular goal in the past, they would need a lot less guidance on what to do. Because they haven't, they require a guide.

EARLY GUIDANCE

I was the recipient of this kind of guidance and investment early in my career at my current company.

About a year into my tenure, a change at the company left my team without a manager, and one of my peers was promoted to the role. It was a choice we all saw coming, and the common belief was that he'd earned the role and was ready for the challenge.

Looking back, he excelled in both areas that are critical to sales leadership: driving sales success and developing the people in his charge.

Over the course of about three years, he did an exceptional job securing contracts with key customers in the absence of a full-time manager in charge of key accounts. Normally, there would have been someone in that role, but various transitions and realignments led to him shouldering the responsibility. His business acumen and execution left a legacy of sales success that far outstretched his time with the company.

Even more important than that, he invested in his people consistently. He prioritized skill and career development in virtually every interaction I had with him.

It was common for us to carve out long lunch breaks in between sales calls to discuss various elements of people leadership. He would come prepared with an exercise for us to walk through or an idea to tackle from all angles.

Under his mentoring, I came to better understand my strengths. I started to recognize what only crystallized later: I not only *preferred* to help others, I was *meant* to do it. I also gained valuable perspective on some ways in which I needed to grow.

One example was that he gave me some visibility into the value of my sales performance.

As a salesperson, I was average at best.

I remember an exercise he walked me through one day. It was the first week of the NCAA's March Madness men's basketball tournament. For the second year in a row, he chose me with whom to make calls on the first day of the tournament and invited me to a long lunch. (This was where we could watch some of the first games of the tournament and use the excuse of my development as our "cover.")

Inevitably, he would actually introduce significant content in support of my development, almost without me realizing it.

On this particular day, he took out a piece of scratch paper and drew something he called a 9-box. I've since learned it is an assessment tool many organizations use to find some variation among employees in their annual calibrations and rankings. It looks something like this:

For the purposes of this story, we can put aside a discussion as to whether this is the *right* tool or not. Some argue that it's an easy way to differentiate between employees for the purpose of awarding differentiated salary increases or considering future promotions or other opportunities. Others argue that this format does not allow for the recognition of elevated performance in certain subgroups.

For example, in this and other similar models, leaders are forced to rank their group and are expected to identify variations in performance — from great to good to average to underperforming. The trouble is that in a high-performing group, you might not have someone who is low in performance, as you might in other groups. Conversely, if a team is underperforming, it may not have a truly differentiated high performer.

Regardless, it was the model our company was using, and a review of our team was the topic of discussion during our fried food and basketball excursion.

He educated me on the model and how it worked. I was unfamiliar with anything like this type of ranking, and the explanation took some time. He was patient with my questions and the slowness of my uptake.

Once some requisite knowledge was established, he asked me to rank our team, including myself. He did recognize up front that I didn't have quite the same perspective he had, but he thought the exercise still had value. I agree.

There was one member of our team who was indisputably great. She belonged in the "9" position — the highest evaluation that could be given. Year in and year out, she continued to prove herself as 9-box material until she learned of a huge professional opportunity outside of our company a year or two later. That was my easy choice for her.

I carefully picked my way through the others. One team member was a consummate high sales performer but did not demonstrate some of the other team and regional leadership attributes that high performers do. I struggled with how to rank that person but settled on a box that was loosely affirmed by my manager.

Then it came to ranking myself. Let's just say that, as compared to his assessment, I drastically overestimated my value to business development compared to my peers.

In my defense, I proved a little naive about others, too. But we could chalk most of that up to my lack of overall visibility of their day-to-day performance.

I learned a huge lesson that day about perspective. I learned lessons about rating and ranking those who report to me. I gained knowledge about the evaluation process and some of the explanations he was asked to give when "proving" our performance to his peers, his boss, and our human resources partners. I garnered new self-awareness. I saw coaching ability demonstrated live and in person.

He proactively generated this exercise as a planned development opportunity for me. I could not have asked for this because I had no knowledge of what it was or how it might be important for my development and my eventual effectiveness as a leader of my own team.

This was just one example of the ways in which this leader showed me the way and then allowed me to demonstrate my self-efficacy and drive in the exercise and the application of those ideas in my ongoing development. He made these learning opportunities part of almost every encounter we had.

I tell my students, 'When you get these jobs that you have been so brilliantly trained for, just remember that your real job is that if you are free, you need to free somebody else. If you have some power, then your job is to empower somebody else. This is not just a grab-bag candy game.'

— **Toni Morrison,** *O,* The Oprah Magazine

This coaching habit hinges on a critical word: facilitate. You might also orchestrate or guide.

WHAT DOES IT MEAN TO TAKE RESPONSIBILITY?

As mentioned previously, some leaders have a hard time distinguishing between leading and driving. The individual must take responsibility for their own development. But what does that mean? It means:

- Being open to coaching
  - The individual is solely responsible for their state of mind and their attitude toward growth. A leader can't make someone want to learn. That must come from a place of self-motivation.
- Doing the work
  - It is not the leader's role to actually do the tasks needed for growth in the individual. This might sound silly as you read it, but this is where some leaders get it wrong. They don't make the distinction between recommending the task and doing the task.
  - The common thing I hear from some leaders is, "If I give them all the answers, then I am doing

the work." I refer them to my house-building analogy.
- Reflecting on their work and learning from it
  - ○ The individual must take the work seriously. It is on them to maximize their experience.

Let's sort this out through an example:

LEADING THE WAY

I was working with a team member, let's call her Aisha, who obviously had the talent, drive, and ability to go anywhere she wanted to in a large corporation like the one we worked for. In just over three years, she'd established herself as a strong salesperson in an industry she was new to.

Partly because it was such a foreign environment to her and partly because it aligned with my leadership philosophy, I quickly led her development to expand her internal contacts and have conversations with people in different roles and in different departments.

Aisha had a tremendous ability to engage different aspects of her personality to meet the needs of those around her (hmm, if this book has taught us anything so far, that is a strong indicator of leadership potential).

For example, our team lacked people who were process- and detail-oriented. This would be someone who leads with blue energy in Insights Discovery or is conscientious in the DiSC model. Aisha regularly stepped in to fill that gap, even though this was just one aspect of her dominant personality and one of her many strengths. She ran reports and manipulated them to be easier to navigate for others. She volunteered to track certain activities when needed.

What's more, she seemed to enjoy the role she played for the team. And, of course, she was good at it.

Our company has an entire department dedicated to pricing strategy and contract management. It was somewhat unusual for someone from sales to work for this team. It wasn't a natural way to move professionally. That said, one of my previous colleagues in sales management now led that department.

I thought that Aisha's attention to detail and her ability to provide structure where structure was needed might be a good match for the work they did.

I set some time with that leader to discuss if there was a way to integrate Aisha into that work on a part-time basis, with the objectives of expanding her network, growing her skill set, and learning more about our business.

I wasn't aware of any openings, and I was unsure how he might feel about engaging my team member. But it was worth a call. I'd always admired him for his dedication to those who reported to him and their personal professional development. If any leader in that position would be up for the conversation, my bet was that he would.

I was right, and it turned out that they were already exploring options to bring in part-time support for a couple of projects.

Remember, at this point in the story, Aisha had (1) very little knowledge of that department, (2) no contacts within that department, and (3) little conviction that this was even an opportunity.

She pursued a role in that department and had an opportunity within days of my call to my colleague. Admittedly, it was less about me being super awesome and more about dumb luck timing. I just happened to call at the exact moment they needed someone.

Yet, if I had not explored that option (based on my projections about her talent, my understanding of the department and possible alignment between her skills and their need, and my relationship with the director of the department), she would not have known to pursue it. She had never "built this house."

If I had not explored that option, she would not have known to pursue it. She had never "built this house."

This brings me to my next point of this story: it was Aisha who did the work of learning new skills and building new career-enriching relationships — *after the idea was put in front of her.*

She absolutely exceeded expectations. She performed over and above what they expected from someone in that position.

Now that she had the role, *she* was accountable for making sure she met its obligations. It was also her responsibility to demonstrate self-efficacy and drive without ideas necessarily coming from an outside source.

Aisha maximized this six-month stint for the purpose of her career. We spoke regularly, and she leaned into leadership there. The conversations centered around making sure her time was well spent from the perspective of her career.

She intentionally reached out to people in other departments and set up calls to learn more about what they do (see the breakout box for more on this tactic). Wherever she could, she'd use the work itself as an excuse to meet or speak.

Aisha excelled in every aspect of the job and moved into another part-time opportunity that came from intentional conversations she'd made earlier. As of this writing, she has been promoted into an exciting role in an altogether different area of the company. This will not be her last move.

> *As a quick aside, if you've never tried proactively setting introduction calls with others, as Aisha did, I highly recommend you try it. It is amazing how many people, at any level and in any role, are willing to give a bit of their time — and it's astounding how much can be gained from it.*
>
> *The development plans of those that I work with often contain the task to connect with X number of people to discuss a specific topic within X number of days or weeks.*
>
> *Here are some tips for setting up these conversations and the why behind each tactic:*
>
> - *Brainstorm first: Make a list of all the people you know of in your sphere of influence who might be interesting to speak with.*
>   - *Why? To expand your thinking. Brainstorming opens your possibilities of connecting to those you might be nervous to approach due to their title, position, personality, etc.*
>   - *Consider people who have skills you desire. Or those who work in an area that is important to your current role or an area you know little about*

but you sense it might help you to know more. Also, list people you think might be decision-makers or advisors in your next steps in the organization.

- *Send invitations: Suggest a thirty-minute meeting. It allows enough time to get to some depth of conversation but isn't too much of an ask, even if your target is very important and busy.*
  - *Why? Because people accept. And if they don't, there is very little risk. If they decline, you can simply move on to the next person on your list. It is highly unlikely that there would be any negative repercussions for simply asking for time.*
  - *Begin by introducing yourself briefly.*
  - *Offer a couple of open-ended questions you would value some perspective on. These questions might be about that person's career path or skills they think are critical to the role. They might be about the operation of the department they are in or their day-to-day responsibilities.*
- *Meet: Come prepared to ask at least three or four open-ended questions on different topics you're curious about.*
  - *Start with the topics you emailed in the invitation, and you may think of others as you prepare for the call.*
  - *Why? Because people like talking about what they know and, in many cases, themselves. I've found this to be true regardless of personality type or personal disposition. We're all starved to be heard. And the higher up in the organization you ascend, the fewer people you have around that you can share ideas with.*

- Listen carefully to what they share and ask deeper questions on those topics as opportunities present themselves. If you demonstrate engagement through open body language and active listening, few will mind extending the conversation.
- Expand: Ask for introductions to other people you should speak with.
  - Why? They probably know better than your leader who you should be speaking with. That's okay. Leaders aren't supposed to know everyone or everything about where you want to go. Their role is to coach you through the process of growth and discovery.
  - Oftentimes, you'll hear a name that hasn't occurred to you. Other times, they recommend a person you have already thought of, but their introduction might make the connection easier and even more worthwhile.
- Keep in touch: Request permission to follow up at regular intervals.
  - Why? You won't know what they might propose until you ask the question. Consistent contact with someone creates the narrative of a career path (we'll discuss narratives later in the book). They'll have a clear history of multiple interactions where you expressed your interest in a certain role or area of the company.
  - With someone critical to your development or if the conversation with them has gone particularly well, you might recommend monthly or quarterly contact.
  - You might also suggest that the two of you reconnect at a specific point in the future, such as when

you apply for that role you discussed or when this project ends, in order to debrief.

- ○ *If follow-up connection isn't needed or wanted for whatever reason, skip this step.*
- *Thank them: At the conclusion of the call and with a quick message or email within twenty-four hours.*
  - ○ *Why? I hope this one's easy to understand — it's a simple sign of respect. It's also a significant demonstration of the importance you put on that encounter.*
- *Follow up: Take action on whatever promises you've made or actions you've pledged to do.*
  - ○ *Why? Follow-through is critical to establishing what that person can expect from you if/when they engage you more. It is remarkable how this differentiates you as a candidate or future colleague. You would think everyone does this. They don't.*

(Please visit mattdickersonvalued.com for a downloadable worksheet that can guide you through this process.)

CASE STUDY – HIPO RETENTION

A few years back, a coaching client came my way. We'll call her Jan in this story.

I was coaching inside a large organization, and Jan jumped right in the first time we met.

"This might be a tough case for you because I don't know what the hell I'm going to do!" Jan didn't waste any time.

I affirmed she was in the right place and asked her to share more.

"I was promoted to my current position about eight months ago. I think I'm producing well, and I'd say that most days, I think I'm staying on top of things. I'm getting good feedback from my leader, and most of my team seems to be doing well despite this being my first leadership role."

It seemed she had yet to share her concern. Then she continued.

"All of that came into question last week in a meeting with my boss." She sank back in her chair and let out a deep breath.

She shared, "He set a call with me, which was kind of out of our normal schedule. I thought something might be up. After exchanging some greetings, he dropped the question on me.

"'How do you think things are going with Edward?'"

This required a little backstory. She explained that Edward was a high-performing member of her team. He had been with the company for seven years — serving in the same role but clearly distinguishing himself with every opportunity and assignment. He had applied for her role when it was posted and was considered by some, including himself, to be the front-runner. In fact, his peers often spoke openly, saying things like, "When you manage this team, Edward, you'll have to ..." Everyone, including Edward, thought the job was his.

Jan continued, "He and I were never on the same team but had worked well together on various projects and initiatives over the years. He's a great guy and a steady performer. And I thought we'd transitioned to boss/employee pretty well.

"And then the conversation with my boss last week."

"How did that go?" I inquired.

"Total surprise! My boss asked, 'Were you aware that Edward is disgruntled and not being shy about sharing it with others?'

"I had no idea! Okay, I knew he was disappointed that he didn't get the role, and I did. I was aware he thought he was the 'next up' and that my applying for the role, much less getting it, was a surprise.

"But all I've done is try to help him since then," she continued. "I've shared any thoughts I have on the projects we're working on, and I've always had an open door for any concerns he had. And I thought we were in a pretty good place."

I asked, "What did your boss suggest?"

She jumped all over that. "He wants *me* to confront Edward about it! I don't know how else to support Edward, and he is apparently not satisfied with that. That's why I'm here. I don't see a path, and I figured a coach couldn't hurt."

We spent some time trying to put Jan in Edward's shoes. How does he really feel about the situation? What's creating those feelings? What does he need right now? How is she seeking to understand and meet those needs? We also brainstormed questions she could ask him when they met.

"Yeah, but I've been putting myself out there for eight months, and this is still my problem?" she quipped.

I gently responded, "Yes, and you might ask yourself: how is it working, and what are the risks and benefits of continuing on in this way?" She conceded a discussion with Edward was in order.

When we met again two weeks later, she updated me on their discussion.

"So, did you have a chance to meet with Edward?" I began.

"I did, and I'm a little surprised by how it went."

Jan had set up a lunch meeting with Edward outside the normal day-to-day. She let him know that this was meant to be informal and that she looked forward to hearing a little more deeply from him.

She decided to put him first.

Once they'd settled in and their food had arrived, she began. "Edward, I was always impressed with your work as a colleague. But it wasn't until I started in this position that I had full visibility of the talents and work ethic you bring to this role and the company. What you contribute is truly re-markable, and I am so thankful to be on this team with you."

She continued. "And it occurs to me I might have rushed into this role and forgot to ask you more about you. That's why I wanted to treat you to lunch and hear more from you. How are you feeling about the current state of affairs — the team, me, your role on the team?"

Edward took a deep breath and put down his fork. He said flatly, "I think things are going okay. I'm good."

This was Jan's opportunity to appeal to him more deeply, and she knew it. She asked, "I appreciate that feedback, and I'm not surprised to hear you say that. You've always been the team player and the 'glass-half-full' leader around here.

"I'm also eager to learn your perspective on where we might be missing the mark. What am I missing? How do I need to improve to help our team achieve more?"

He took another breath and seemed hesitant to speak. Jan gave him space in that moment. "Let him process," she told herself.

After what seemed like an hour but was likely under a minute, Edward offered, "If I'm being honest, I really thought I was going to get your role. I got very little feedback after I was passed over, and I don't have a clear idea of what my next step is or how I can achieve it."

Jan was surprised that just a couple of questions could bring out this kind of insight. And she was ready to receive it. "Edward, that seemed like an important thing to share, and I so appreciate you trusting me with your thoughts," she responded. "Could you tell me a bit more about that?"

"It's no slam on you, Jan. I think you're very accomplished, and I admire you for the many things you do here. I just thought I had a clear path, and now I don't know where I'm going. I guess I just don't have a good idea of where I need to improve or what that's going to get me."

Jan was processing. "Again, I appreciate you sharing. This is what I was hoping to get into more detail with you now. My perception is that I regularly make myself available to the members of the team. I'm constantly trying to find ways to share my knowledge about our process and products." She could feel herself getting defensive, and she knew that wasn't the right call right now. From our discussion, she knew she had to leave herself open to what he had to say and give space for him to pace the conversation.

He responded carefully, "And I appreciate those things, Jan, I really do. But I'm pretty equipped to deal with the technical aspects of the role. What I'm lacking right now is career direction." He went on, "Listen, this company has given me so much. I want to be here. But I need to know that there's a future. I need to know where I'm going and how I can put myself in the best position to get there." He added somewhat reluctantly, "And that's what I need your help on."

Jan spent the rest of our time together that day describing the impact that this encounter had on her. "You know," she said, "just a couple of well-placed questions, and I got a whole other side of Edward. I have so much more clarity on who I need to be for him and how I can help him in the areas *he* needs help in. Can it really be that easy?"

Over the course of many months, Edward was an infrequent topic in our coaching sessions until one day, near the end of my engagement with Jan, she scheduled an impromptu call.

"Matt, you won't believe it!"

She had my attention.

"You remember that team member, Edward?"

"Of course! It's been a while since he's come up, but yes, we spent some time on him in the early sessions, didn't we?"

"Yes!" she exclaimed. "He got promoted last week and is leading another team in our business unit!"

"That's great news!" I responded, reacting to her obvious excitement.

She caught me up. "If you remember, he and I had that lunch together where we got to the bottom of his concern and also my role in it. You and I haven't discussed him much because, after that lunch, everything changed.

"In our next one-on-one, we brainstormed and got down on paper all the concerns he had about the changes going on and his role and future in them. I asked *him* what small steps he might want to take to fill in some of his gaps here. He had great ideas! I was able to provide a thought here or there, but the plan was mostly his.

"He began to reach out to others in and outside the company who could speak to his development plan. I lobbied my boss for some more specific feedback on Edward and what he was missing in consideration for the promotion.

"He and I met regularly to revisit his plan and plot next steps. And again, he was the main generator of ideas. I just tried to ask good questions to help him think about things from different perspectives. I provided advice where needed, but my focus wasn't on sharing my wisdom. I embraced my role of 'coach.'

"Which leads us to last week. Edward was approached by a vice president in another business unit. They'd had a couple of calls in the previous months (a part of his development plan). She had a new leader position open on her team. She reached out to him!" Her excitement was palpable.

"Shortly after, Edward was offered the role, and he accepted."

"That's incredible!" I responded. "How does that make you feel about your work with him?"

And then she spoke the moral of this story, the meaning of the parable. "You know, it all changed the second I stopped having all the answers and started asking questions." Hmm. "I'd been so focused on sharing my knowledge, overseeing the tactical aspects of the role, and managing that I overlooked my opportunity to just show up and ask questions."

Jan was facilitating Edward's growth, but Edward was doing the work. And they were both better for it!

If you were Jan in this scenario, what do you think would be your responsibility to model for those working for you, like Edward? We'll explore that next!

CHAPTER 6

COACHING HABIT #4
MODELING GROWTH

Habit Is Seen As: Role Model
Value or Belief Behind this Habit: You Don't Have to Do It Alone

> Knowing who in fact we are results in Good Being, and Good Being
> results in the most appropriate kind of good doing.
> **— Aldous Huxley**

I often say, half-joking, that I have a long history of being in rooms I never should have been in. And, like with all good jokes, there's some truth to it. I've been invited to participate in numerous projects and new opportunities that exceeded my current capabilities or the opportunities I "should" be given at that point in my career (we discussed the dangers of "should" a few chapters back).

BEING IN THE WRONG ROOM... THAT ENDED UP BEING THE RIGHT ONE

Stark among the examples is the time I was invited to join a cohort of twelve who would be trained as internal executive coaches within the large organization for which I worked. My company was expending a not-insignificant amount of money to send me through a program normally reserved for higher-level employees with a career focus on talent development or human resources.

While it's been almost five years, I can still remember walking into that conference room in a nondescript office building somewhere in New Jersey on the first day of coach certification training.

I'd flown in the night before and woke up that morning with a "What in the world makes me think I can do this?" anxiety that followed me to the building that day.

As I pressed the button in the elevator to go to the second floor, I actually had the thought, "I wonder if they're going to allow me to participate. Or, once I get there and they double check their rosters, are they going to realize their mistake and politely let me know there's been a mistake?"

I entered the room uneasily and quickly went to the coffee station. "Ah, getting coffee. This is a normal thing to do and will help me act like I belong here." And then someone else came to get coffee! "Uh-oh," I thought. "It would be weird if I didn't say something or introduce myself, but how quickly do I want to be exposed for the imposter that I am?"

"Good morning," I blurted out before my nerves got the best of me. "I'm Matt, nice to meet you." They shared their name and a similar greeting.

Now what? "Don't panic; you're used to talking to people," I reminded myself. "Just. Talk."

"I assume you're with (my company). What do you do?"

Dumb and dumb. Of course, we were from the same company. The cohort was made up of internal employees. And "What do you do?" That's exactly the discussion I didn't want to get into! If I asked them that, they were likely to ask me the same question, and then the gig was up!

"I'm a director of HR in X division," she answered easily. "What about you?" she casually shot back.

"Well, okay, I guess we'll get this started and see how it goes," I thought before answering, "I'm a sales manager in vaccines."

I couldn't read the look on her face. Confusion? Amusement? Indifference?

"Oh, really? Great! Nice to meet you!"

I was as surprised as I was relieved. "Maybe I can make this work. Maybe I can at least survive the first day."

After a few minutes, we were all ushered into the conference room to begin. I looked around the room. I recognized one person as the chief of staff for the head of HR for all of North America. One was the company's primary employee relations contact, covering nearly 30,000 employees. Everyone in that room outranked me by at least two levels in our company. All of them not only had people leadership responsibilities but also had roles that were solely about talent development or human resources. What was some chump from sales doing sitting in this room?

Slowly, in the coming weeks and months, I learned that I did belong there. I brought my curiosity and a healthy dose of humility to the lessons and exercises and learned things about myself and others that I could not have foreseen.

That experience was transformative for me in so many ways and is a big reason you are even reading this book. Without the self-understanding gained over the next six-plus months and the encouragement of my fellow cohort members, I would not have the clarity of thought and purpose I have today.

So, what's the lesson? How do you think this experience equipped me to lead well going forward? I stretched myself way beyond what I thought I had earned or what I could tackle. And it was a success. Modeling Growth is critical to leading others in their growth.

Modeling Growth is critical to leading others in their growth.

 COACHING HABIT #4 – MODELING GROWTH

HABIT IS SEEN AS: ROLE MODEL
VALUE OR BELIEF BEHIND THIS HABIT: YOU DON'T HAVE TO DO IT ALONE

I've told some form of that story dozens of times. It's one of my best examples of doing a lot of the right things to be invited to participate in something that stretches us.

I share because this story can be a vehicle for pointing out many best practices in self-growth. I share because it is an example that proves to others that I'm doing for myself what I am preaching. I share because the rewards of that experience have been so numerous, long-lasting, and life-changing that it is an amazing example of what fruit can come from the growth process.

It leads to discoveries like one I heard from a colleague at another company. Here's her recount:

WALKING THE WALK

Rory was a senior leader at a finance company. She had been in her current role for several years and with the company for over fifteen years. She had earned multiple promotions and awards for her work and was generally highly regarded.

She was meeting with a direct report, Stephon, who was considered high-potential but was missing ... something.

> I asked Stephon to join me for an impromptu lunch. As we sat down with our food at the company cafe, I attempted to engage Stephon in a career conversation.
>
> "Stephon," I began, "I think I tell you this often, but I'm so appreciative of your work on this team. You make me and those around you better on a daily basis. Our team would not have achieved the success we have recently without your technical skill and collaborative work."
>
> "Thanks, Rory. I enjoy working on this team, and I appreciate your leadership as well." He

seemed genuine, and I wasn't surprised by his answer.

"I do wonder what might be next professionally for you," I continued.

Stephon thought about it for a moment. I thought I knew what he was going to say. I thought he'd say something like he was satisfied with where he was at. I was right.

"Honestly, Rory, I'm enjoying my role and the team, as I just shared. I'm pretty content doing what I'm doing."

I was prepared for this. Or I thought I was.

I shared, "Stephon, I am glad to hear that. Feeling good about your work is very important to me. I also wonder what we might do to challenge you further or stretch you in your development. Any thoughts?"

He said, "I'm always interested in getting better. I do feel like this role is still a daily challenge for me. I'm learning new things and feel engaged."

"Again," I encouraged, "I'm pleased to hear that. I was curious if this was an area that I might push you a little in. While it's clear you excel in this role, I also think you have much more opportunity to accomplish other things with our company, and I'd like to support that."

"Yeah," he said cautiously, "I don't know what that might be. I think maybe it would be best for me to continue to dive into this team and these projects. I don't think there's anything wrong with that."

"I don't, either," I shot back quickly. Admittedly, I could feel the "but" in my tone. "And ... I want to challenge you to do more."

He thought about it for a moment. As he shifted in his seat and diverted his eye contact, I could tell he was uncomfortable.

"I certainly trust you on this and am willing to take on other things if it helps." I was glad for this response and wasn't quite prepared for what was next. "I wonder," he continued, "what kinds of projects or stretch assignments have you done in the past year or two? Is there something you've done that you would recommend for me?"

And there it was. The truth was that I had not done much outside of my current role for at least eighteen months. I wasn't lazy or apathetic. I wasn't disengaged. I guess I just had not been purposeful about seeking out new opportunities.

And then it hit me: I was Stephon in this instance. He had just shared with me that he enjoyed his role, his team, and his boss. He felt like his work mattered, and he felt valued. He felt challenged daily and didn't see an immediate need to do more.

That was my story, too.

I realized in that moment that I was not heeding my own advice. I had to do some soul-searching. Was I right about continuous development and needed to self-coach my way to my next challenge? Or, did I need to reevaluate my position on growth, even if my professional world is going well?

> **I realized in that moment that I was not heeding my own advice.**

Ultimately, I came to the conclusion that I wasn't living into the values I was always talking about. I was not challenging myself in a way that modeled what I expected of others on my team.

I appreciate Rory's story for her candid disclosure and also for her ability to self-assess on something as important as people development. This was a good example of how easy it is to fall into a pattern that unintentionally stifles progress in those we lead.

 ## COACHING HABIT #4 – MODELING GROWTH

HABIT IS SEEN AS: ROLE MODEL
VALUE OR BELIEF BEHIND THIS HABIT: YOU DON'T HAVE TO DO IT ALONE

In my fifteen-plus years as a people leader, I have a history of favoring candidates in the interview process who have (1) less experience and (2) differentiated professional curiosity. The first attribute is tricky, especially in sales. Without substantial sales success historically, what data point do I have that suggests that they will sell at a high level in our organization? The second attribute is nebulous and hard to quantify. It is also subject to conscious and unconscious bias and, therefore, should always be questioned.

However, I've found this to be a winning formula, generally. I've been fortunate to be a part of teams in an organization that embraces and rewards curiosity. Without bad habits to break, candidates newer to the sales process can be trained in a way that best aligns with our business needs and their personal strengths.

An important distinction here is that I'm not only referring to candidates early in their careers. I'll share an example in support of this point.

THE CALCULATED RISK

Some years ago, I took a calculated chance on a candidate, let's call her Yvonne, who I later learned was in her late forties. She'd been in sales for twenty years but in industries far from the science and regulation of pharmaceutical and medical sales. She was able to demonstrate repeated sales success, but in an environment that had very little parallel to what we did, day-to-day.

I recall a conversation I had with one of her teammates, whom I had asked to be her primary peer mentor and help Yvonne adjust. Let's call him Enrique for this story.

"So, Matt, I have a concern about Yvonne." I was anticipating this conversation because whispers of concerns had already made their way back to me.

"I just don't think Yvonne gets it," Enrique continued. "How so?" I asked, trying to leave some space for him to share, even though I thought I had a pretty good idea of what he was going to say.

"Well, she's really struggling with the limitations of our industry. She has been selling in the 'Wild, Wild, West' for two decades, and she's not used to so much direction and so many restrictions. She keeps coming up with new ideas that don't fit what we've been instructed to do. I don't think she understands the potential consequences of some of the tactics she's using."

"What's the conversation been like so far with her?" I asked.

"Well, every time she brings something to me, I'm quick to share the risk or tell her that she can't do that. But she reminds me that she's been selling for years and knows how to change customer behavior."

I took a moment to remind myself that my role here was to first try to help Enrique solve this concern through his own skills and emotional intelligence (he had both in spades).

"What is she doing that you think is unique and *could* fit our model and expectations?"

He offered an example. "Well, she's very good about following up with the customers. She sends an email after almost every sales call. In it, she'll confirm something the customer asked her to follow up on, if appropriate. The real new thing is that she briefly recaps aspects of the conversation that she thinks she might need to repeat with the customer."

"Good, something to build on," I thought but did not say out loud. I did say, "That sounds like a solid tactic. What's her reasoning for doing that?"

"I think it's to make sure she and the customer took the same things away from the conversation," he responded.

"That's really smart. What, if anything, have you shared with her about that tactic? What did that conversation sound like?" I led further.

"I actually had a chance to mention it briefly during our call with each other a couple of days ago, but I don't think I'd fully processed how different her approach there was."

"What do you think you could say to her about this topic next time?"

He thought about it for a moment. "What I really appreciate about her approach is that it helps break down the important parts of the conversation she just had with the customer. It happens too often that I leave a customer thinking that we'd decided something or were clear on an idea, only to find out the next time I speak with them that they took something completely different from the conversation."

"I like that," I responded encouragingly. "How could you position that praise within the context of challenging her, too, to 'stay in bounds' in other areas?"

I could tell he was really processing. I gave him a minute.

"I think it could help me have a more balanced conversation with her."

"How so?"

"Well, I could set up the conversation from the perspective of her bringing some new ideas to the table that I've never thought about. And then, I can revisit a message of, 'It's my responsibility to keep you safe and let you know when a tactic is new and good or simply outside of something we can do.'"

"How would you layer that into this particular tactic?"

"As I think through it, I'd like to share that these follow-up emails are good for confirming items discussed on the calls. I could also share some examples of things that should not be put into the emails for legal reasons. I could help her with the do's and don'ts of sending emails in a highly regulated industry. She's just not used to that."

Bingo! Enrique had talked himself into a solution. And as it turned out, he did have that conversation with Yvonne. Several times!

Yvonne eventually settled into a compromise between her creativity and our constraints and achieved significant sales success. When her family had to relocate to another state, she left the team with tears and a history of success.

This habit is formed in the belief that you don't have to do it alone.

I was not solely responsible for this new employee's success. I had equipped a capable peer mentor through asking him good questions.

DOING AT THE EXPENSE OF LEADING

Many leaders, early in their people-leading experience, can fall into the trap of "doing" as opposed to "leading." They miss the chance to enable others to help themselves and their teams.

Marc, a senior research leader at a global cosmetics company, recounted a story in our survey results:

> *"When I first started leading a team, I thought I had to make every decision and be part of every-thing. This makes your team feel micromanaged and useless. After a few months, a couple members of my team told me point-blank that they were tired of it and told me to back off. At the*

*time, I was confused/hurt, but in retrospect, prob-
ably the best thing that ever happened to me."*

I can, in truth, probably claim just a small percentage of
what my team members achieved in their years with us. A
great deal of credit goes to the individual, of course. Yvonne,
from the previous example, had a tremendous work ethic
and was a great person to be around. She was smart, dedicated, and driven.

She was also surrounded by a cocoon of support. Enrique
was just one (although quite an important one) of the many
who rallied around Yvonne throughout her career. She had
countless people she could call for answers, support, tough
love, rich discussion, or challenge.

What I can take some credit for, as a leader, is cultivating
an environment where this type of supportive behavior is
encouraged — almost expected. I can also take some credit
for helping each individual understand and grow in the way
they mentor and guide.

Yvonne's story is a good example of this principle. As we
saw in Chapter 3 (Coaching Habit #1 - Focusing on Others),
asking strong, open-ended questions allows us as leaders to
guide someone to their own answers. In my conversation
with Enrique, I tried to stay curious longer.

As Michael Bungay Stanier points out in his fundamentally important book, *The Advice Trap*, we can follow three
simple coaching principles.

- Be lazy
- Be curious
- Be often

Explained simply, being lazy is being slow to chime in. Being often is incorporating coaching and listening tactics into *every* conversation you have, as opposed to pulling it out as a special tool for a unique occasion.

The middle principle, be curious, is what I was attempting to embody in this conversation. Did I have ideas about how this could be handled? Sure! Did I have a sense of how it might turn out? Absolutely! Did I have a responsibility to guide my team member through a conversation where they self-discovered their own way of working through the issue? *Yes!*

Enrique left our conversation not only better equipped to confront this specific issue, but he'd also built some muscle memory for how to handle it — or something like it — in the future.

If I did my job well that day, I helped him help me. I supported him in a way that he could then take future work and responsibility off my plate. I taught him how to peer mentor more effectively.

Since that conversation, Enrique has been hugely influential as a mentor in the ongoing success of our team and the development of many new hires and struggling teammates. It would be difficult for me to quantify the number of hours he's saved me, in addition to the actual impact he's had on others.

ENSURING FUTURE SUCCESS

The point is that by equipping others, I increase the probability of our future collective success and decrease the amount of oversight and time I need to spend in order to make that happen.

In the polling I did as research for this book, I frequently saw feedback on how hard it is or would be to lead people. I saw concerns about how much time people would have to spend bringing up others' skills to minimum expectations or "cleaning up others' messes." Coaching my team members to increase their capabilities to coach their peers has been critical to whatever success I've achieved as a people leader. Here are a few quotes directly from the survey:

> *"I have no interest in managing others. I don't think I would want to put up with 'babysitting adults.'"*

> *"I don't want the hassle and responsibility."*

> *"I love to help walk alongside people and help them in a way that is consistent with what I believe a manager should do. However, because of the reality of what 'management/ leadership' usually becomes, I have no interest in actually pursuing a position that is a formal leadership role."*

Going back to my hiring criteria, what is the probability that I could do that successfully if I was solely responsible for the development of those new hires? Not high. Not because I don't possess the skills and the passion for helping them achieve their goals. I would be far less successful if I had to do it on my own because there simply are not enough hours in the day!

I can take chances on less-qualified candidates because I have a team capable of building them up. And we have a culture that helps them naturally be that person to the next new hire.

As we will discuss in Chapter 8 (Coaching Habit #6 – Driving Results), hiring "riskier" candidates with higher upsides can have significant benefits for the team, internal and external customers, and the company as a whole. You can lead a team that becomes a feeder system for other departments and functions within the company.

In *The Catalyst Effect*, Jerry Toomer and his colleagues summarized their research where they sought to quantify and catalog what attributes or competencies leaders share. What makes a leader, if not status or title?

One of the cornerstones their research revealed was what they called "amplifying impact." They suggest that:

> *The work associated with amplifying impact is embedded in the team and organizational stories that become the fabric of an organization's culture. How do we drive an uncompromising approach to excellence? Who successfully mentors and coaches our up-and-coming talent? What imaginative ideas emerge to drive innovation and ensure sustainable organizational success?*[5]

They identified that leaders who excel in amplifying impact, regardless of title or position, are behaviorally differentiated in three core competencies:

- Pursues excellence
- Mentors and coaches others to excel
- Proposes imaginative solutions

Toomer and his co-researchers define the second competency — mentors and coaches — as being one who "models exemplary behavior and supports the personal and professional development of others by providing constructive feedback."

I love this characterization because it centers on modeling *exemplary* behavior.

Within the context of people leadership, it is our responsibility to model the behaviors that we would like to see of others in the support of their peers and other stakeholders.

As a people leader with a title (a manager), you can amplify your own impact by teaching your team members what good mentoring and coaching look like and equipping them to be that support to others in your place. When it comes to coaching, you don't have to do it alone.

CHAPTER 7

COACHING HABIT #5
REFLECTING AND ACKNOWLEDGING

Habit Is Seen As: Actively Engaged
Value or Belief Behind This Habit: Being Present is Important

Managers assert drive and control to get things done; leaders
pause to discover new ways of being and achieving.
— **Dan Pontefract**, *The Purpose Effect*

The desire to overwork is an attempt to justify ourselves. For many,
there is a connection between our overachieving and our desire
to prove our self-worth. Our overcompensating becomes a way to
validate our existence. We pour ourselves into our surroundings, into
our people, and into our agendas. We add to the productivity, the
creativity, and the humanity of our world, and we do so with a hidden
soul-level motive. If we can do enough, we can be enough.
— **Saundra Dalton-Smith**, *Sacred Rest*

How often do you stop to take stock of what is really happening?

How often do you pause before acting or responding?

How routine is it for you to carve out time in a conversation, in your day, or over the course of a week or month to simply absorb all the data you are being bombarded with?

How often do you "give space"?

360 TOOLS

There are countless types of 360 tools on the market.

If you're not familiar with them, 360 assessments contain a series of questions that are meant to assess or rate an individual's ability to execute various skills and attributes of leadership. These questions are most often both quantitative ("Rate this person on a scale of 1 to 10") and qualitative ("What could this leader do better or what should they do less of?"). Different tools highlight different skills, tendencies, abilities, and competencies. However, they all focus on attributes that most would readily identify as important for workplace leadership and success, such as strategy, vision, collaboration, analysis, and emotional intelligence.

They're referred to as a 360 because, if executed correctly, it involves various stakeholders in a "360-degree view" around one individual. The participant invites their boss or bosses, their peers, their colleagues, and/or their direct reports to answer these questions. They also take the assessment, rating themselves on the same questions.

These tools are used in several different ways. Ideally, they're done with some regularity and/or for the purpose of the professional development of that individual. In less than ideal situations, they're deployed where corrective action is in place or predicted in the near future "if something doesn't change."

For the latter reason, 360s sometimes come with baggage. Many have preconceived and possibly negative notions about what they are and aren't and what they're intended for.

While there are several effective versions, the ones that seem to be the most effective are those that encourage reflection as a part of the process. As opposed to other 360s, where the participant is provided with feedback and quickly ushered into developing an action plan for addressing or fixing the issues.

The best companion to a 360 process is a certified coach to usher you through it. A coach can be critical to sifting through the massive amounts of information these reports produce about you. A coach can help you discover what themes jump out to you, where you should focus your developmental energy, and what information you might be right to simply let go of.

In the absence of a coach, some 360 tools are better than others at encouraging and equipping self-reflection. One tool I have used often was created by The Catalyst Effect (*https://www.thecatalysteffect.org*) and is available to coaches for work with their clients. It's called action360 (*https://www.action360.us/*), and it's designed to meet the need for a pause — a time to reflect, a chance to digest.

It has no fewer than twelve pages that ask thoughtful, largely open-ended questions in the areas and competencies that are focused on in the report. Participants can use these pages as well as worksheets provided at the back of the report to take themselves through a thorough reflection.

If someone does not have the opportunity to process what this information means to them fully, it's unlikely they'll be able to effectively develop and execute a plan to work on the right things.

GUIDING A 360 PARTICIPANT TO CONSTRUCTIVE CONCLUSIONS

A couple of years ago, I was working with an internal client — let's call him Jim — who had recently been led through an interview-based 360. This method is often used only with leaders higher in an organization because they are (1) very labor-intensive and (2) allow for much deeper insights due to the ability of the interviewer to ask follow-up questions.

In this scenario, a coach or a consultant would conduct 30- or 60-minute interviews with the same stakeholders described above. They would take notes, compile their information, and use it in support of their work with the assigned leader — in this case, Jim.

Jim was deeply affected by the feedback and was struggling to wrap his head around what he should do with it. I was not a part of the process but felt compelled to guide him in the absence of another resource being provided for him.

Imagine you were in Jim's shoes. You've just been given pointed feedback, and some of it is completely surprising. Much of it is negative. You've learned you are showing up to your colleagues in a way that doesn't align with who you want to be.

The report was pages and pages of typed feedback. It was arranged so that all or most of the notes the consultant took were grouped below the question he asked each stakeholder. The consultant interviewed twenty-two people! It was a *long* report and a lot for Jim to digest.

"How long have you had the report?" I first asked.

"About twenty-four hours," he responded. He wasn't hiding his struggle. "I had my 'debrief' with the consultant yesterday afternoon." He used air quotes as if to express his lack of enthusiasm for whatever had happened.

I nodded.

"The problem is," he continued, "that there is so much information, I feel like most of it is negative, and my boss is already emailing me asking for my action plan."

To provide perspective, Jim was matched with me as a coach because he is widely considered in his area of our company to be a rising star. He is being introduced to tools like the 360 and coaching with me as a reward for his hard work and in recognition of the promising future he has in front of him. This is probably not the employee the boss should be browbeating about an urgent action plan.

"Perhaps we could review it together," I offered. "We could use our time together to help you process the information." He quickly agreed and shared his document through the Zoom screen.

I asked him, "As you read through the report, which of these questions did you think was the most important?"

"What do you mean?"

"Which of these questions did you read and think, 'Yep, that's an important one to tackle,' or 'Okay, at least they're asking about that aspect'?"

"Ah, got it," and he gave it some thought. "I think the one I was most interested in was the one about what people valued about working with me. I was really curious about what they might say."

"Great!" I said. "Do you think that specific question might be a good place to start our review?"

He nodded in agreement.

"What statements here resonated with you, either because they made you curious or confused or because you had the sense that they were important?"

He dove deep into thought. "Well, when I look back through it now, it's a bit surprising!"

"How so?"

"Well, it's not like I'm trying to brag, but I thought there would be a lot of positive comments about my technical skill." He served as a CFO for one of our larger business units. And there *was* lots of praise and appreciation for what technical skills he brought to the table. He acknowledged that and continued. "But what I'm surprised about is how many comments involve ... I don't know ... like emotional support."

He smiled faintly, and I gave a slight smile in response. I said, "You know, I was noticing that too as you were scrolling through. How much stock do you put in those comments?"

"Well, a lot. I'm part of a very collaborative team that performs at a high level. These comments suggest that they think I'm important in that."

I confirmed, "Yeah, I see at least two comments about you being the glue, and someone even called you the 'mother hen of the team but in a good way.'" We both laughed at that.

And then we both went very quiet.

He had his head pointed slightly down, and as he raised it slowly, I was surprised to see the beginning of tears in his eyes.

"What are you feeling?" I asked carefully.

"I guess sometimes it's just really hard to know what people really think about you. And I'm not the best with emotion and reading emotion in others. I like to think that I'm being supportive because that's really important to me. But ..."

Space.

"But," he went on, "I guess I have a lot of doubt because I always have to be the police in our meetings. I'm the guy that asks a lot of questions and says no. As the CFO, I don't have the luxury to walk in the gray much. I try to compensate by being open to discussion, and I probably go out of my way to appear friendly and approachable."But who knows if it's working."

"Until now," I offered.

"Until now," he repeated.

"So, what do you make of that?" I extended. There was clarity to be gained here, but I didn't think he was going to see it right away. But he did.

"Well, if this is what many of my peers actually think of me, I can probably use it to my advantage. Could I really chalk this up to a strength of mine?"

I nodded my head exaggeratedly. "Yep," I said simply.

My client had a superpower that he was not fully aware of until this experience. Now that he had the "proof" and he was able to label that strength, we could use it to guide the work he wanted to do in his development plan.

We spent the rest of our time that day and our entire next session wrestling with an action plan that prominently featured his strengths and used them as tools for development in other areas he and his boss agreed to.

Within two weeks, he had a plan that was aligned with what his boss wanted him to focus on, one that he could be proud of and that was entirely actionable for him. Without reflection and acknowledgement, my client would have not only struggled in the short term to respond to the 360 feedback in an appropriate way, but he could have also suffered longer-term self-doubt or resentment toward his team or any host of other possible negative outcomes.[6]

> **Without reflection and acknowledgement, my client would have not only struggled in the short term to respond to the 360 feedback in an appropriate way, but he could have also suffered longer-term self-doubt or resentment toward his team or any host of other possible negative outcomes.**

 COACHING HABIT #5 – REFLECTING AND ACKNOWLEDGING

HABIT IS SEEN AS: ACTIVELY ENGAGED
VALUE OR BELIEF BEHIND THIS HABIT: BEING PRESENT IS IMPORTANT

As I write this book, we are finding new patterns for our professional lives in the aftermath of the COVID-19 pandemic. Much has already been written about the challenges of communication and team trust and rapport during that period, which provided so many lessons about what good and bad leadership look like.

Truth be told, we are still adapting.

But what does it look like to be seen as actively engaged?

As you might expect, responses to the leadership survey that preceded this book were peppered with COVID-related stories. Being actively engaged (or not) with your team members was chief among the examples.

One respondent, Neil, a leader at a large healthcare organization, shared:

> *"During COVID, my direct leader checked out. They decided they could lead from home, rarely checked in on me, and were never on the front lines. On the rare occasion they had to come into work, they were very vocal that this was a huge burden. It demonstrated that they were willing to lead during good times but were only interested in what worked best for them during challenging times."*

Neil provides an unfortunate example of what active engagement does *not* look like.

Being completely absent and aggressively negative, like Neil's leader, isn't the only way to lack an appearance of being actively engaged with your employees.

Sometimes, it's about being busy doing so many other "important" things that we miss the chance to pause, assess, reflect, and respond. Let's look at how we may find our leadership being up to "PARR" (see what I did there!).[7]

PAUSE, ASSESS, REFLECT, RESPOND

Pause

To "pause" can take many shapes. Kevin Cashman covers this comprehensively in his brilliant book, *The Pause Principle*. In Chapter 2 (Pause to Grow Personal Leadership), he shares this:

> *"Pausing to find our deepest values and bringing them to all our domains of leadership may be the most crucial aspect of our development as whole leaders."*[8]

In the context of leading well, pausing is very much about allowing space that is unscripted and under-planned.

This could look like scheduling a brief meeting with a team member and allowing them to drive the conversation to the topics *they'd* prefer to focus on.

It could look like — even in that same conversation — giving space for your team member to process in that moment, allowing silence or being patient with repeat points or thoughts.

Survey respondent Anabelle gave a touching example of giving space as a leader, with her being the recipient in this example:

> *"The best experience to whom I reported was during my personal crisis and trying to meet the high demand of my new role. My manager demonstrated empathy and listened to my needs. He allowed me to come up with a solution. I was able to be available to my child's medical needs and my teammates*

*who supported me throughout the year. I was able
to meet the business needs with my team's support.*"

Her boss listened to her needs and allowed her to come up with a solution. They provided the space for Anabelle to be heard and also to come up with her own answer to the problem. Evidently, it was one they could agree on, and it successfully allowed her to navigate between what she needed to be for the team and also for her family.

This would not have been possible without some element of *pause*.

Assess

Assessing a situation is frequently where we, as leaders and capable professionals, can lean on our expertise and so-called hard skills. What is happening here, and how does my depth of experience and knowledge apply to this circumstance? What part of this am I equipped to weigh in on if I'm needed? If I do need to share an opinion or guidance, how important or urgent is this concern?

This is also a great place to employ "softer" skills. Fortunately, because of our dive into personalities in Chapter 4 (Coaching Habit #2 – Recognizing What's Needed of You) and meeting people where they are in Chapter 3 (Coaching Habit #1 – Focusing on Others), we are now better able to do this.

As we learned from Coaching Habit #1, when we focus on others, it is based on the core belief/value that it's about them.

For example, if the person sharing is more prone to value discussion and thoughtful processing, we can use that data to *assess* what role we're meant to play in this conversation.

If they appreciate talking things through, part of our assessment is to remind ourselves of that trait and how that might factor into our next steps.

I've built into my routine at this assessment step to frequently ask, "As you share this thought, what do you need from me?" My team members have become fairly accustomed to this question now. But before we developed that muscle memory, I would proactively cue them with a few options: "Would you like to vent? Do you need my help solving this problem? Or are you hoping to talk it through with me as a sounding board?"

Reflect

The first part of this chapter gave us a good example of the power of reflection guided by a coach.

Reflection most often comes in the form of someone carving out dedicated time to sit with new information and/ or some ongoing feelings.

In today's fast-paced life, where many of us have every minute of every day scheduled out, this can be easy to overlook and undervalue.

The truth is, with careful reflection comes more informed decisions. More informed decisions increase the probability of success and positive outcomes.

> **The truth is, with careful reflection comes more informed decisions. More informed decisions increase the probability of success and positive outcomes.**

Respond

This fourth step generally comes easily to many of us, particularly if we're experts in an area or passionate about the topic.

If preceded by the three other steps listed above, your response in communication is more likely to be (1) measured, (2) informed, and (3) balanced.

Attitudinal assessments like the Energy Leadership Index and Positive Intelligence[9] are most helpful in understanding our initial reaction and also controlling what happens next and/or how long we "sit in" the initial feeling or emotion. Put simply, if we stub our toe, we often can't help our reaction in that first two seconds of pain. We may shout or curse or bang our fist on something nearby. But, as these programs help us understand, we completely control what we do after that initial reaction — our response.

Pausing, assessing, and reflecting allows us to respond in a way that best aligns with who we are and who we want to be.

 COACHING HABIT #5 – REFLECTING AND ACKNOWLEDGING

HABIT IS SEEN AS: ACTIVELY ENGAGED
**VALUE OR BELIEF BEHIND THIS HABIT: BEING PRESENT
IS IMPORTANT**

BEING BUSY VERSUS BEING PRESENT

As a less-experienced leader, I often found myself wrapped up in "being busy." Have you ever found yourself in a similar situation?

Maybe you've been legitimately trying to tackle multiple pressing issues at once. Perhaps you've had seasons where personnel issues, administrative tasks, and business needs all seem to converge to be critical all at the same time.

It's also true that in other seasons, you may have just thought you were busy or were trying to be busy. Have there been times when ego or self-worth was tied to how busy you thought you were?

I'll admit that I've not completely tackled this particular part of my personality. A lot of my professional identity is wrapped up in how many things are expected of me at any given time.

There is an obvious cost to this, although it was not always obvious to me at the time. Because I was so wrapped up in competing priorities and checking my email a thousand times a day (as just one of many bad habits), I was rarely truly present with others.

I remember one meeting in particular ...

WHEN YOU'RE JUST BUSY

Several years ago, I was on a temporary assignment in another department of my company. It's common in my company for employees to be given an opportunity to expand their skill set through fixed-time assignments in other areas or functions. This is one of the many ways in which I am thankful for the company I have spent nearly twenty years with.

During those "rotations," as we often refer to them, it's also common for someone else, looking to build skill or try out a new role, to fill in for your role.

While in one of those rotations, my schedule permitted me to attend a two-day meeting with my team, with someone else leading them. I had no responsibility for conducting or contributing to the meeting. I used that as an excuse to be disconnected from and not present for the interpersonal interactions over the course of the two days.

I was visibly distracted and disinterested in what was being discussed. In retrospect, it was clear that I was a hindrance to the productiveness of the meeting. I also found out later that there were repairs I needed to make to individual relationships in that group.

This was an example of missing a critical belief of good leadership: being present is important!

Presence is not just actual attendance — being in the room, so to speak.

Presence is being mentally and emotionally there. It is intentionally putting away distractions. Presence is shown through body language as well as vocal communication. Presence is essential in establishing trust and rapport with others. Being fully present demonstrates respect for others.

WHEN YOU'RE TRULY PRESENT IN THE MIDST OF "BUSY"

This reminds me of a coaching session I led near the beginning of my coaching journey.

The client was a chief of staff for a critical function within a large organization. We'll call her Marsha.

We'd met for two or three sessions at this point, and we were still working through how our time together might be most useful.

I don't recall the exact specifics of why I felt so hurried and overwhelmed that day, but it likely had something to do with the many hats I was wearing in the organization at the time. Coaching was a very small part of my role, and most of my priorities were aligned with leading a sales team. This coaching session "interrupted" my other duties, and today, it was *feeling* like an interruption.

We met via Zoom, as always, and Marsha and I joined at the same time.

Normally, I try to carve out at least five or ten minutes prior to a coaching session to review my notes from previous sessions and center myself in a coaching mindset. This day, I was running from commitment to commitment with no time to collect myself. Chances are, you can identify with that.

Thankfully, in that moment, I had the presence of mind to take myself through some quick techniques that help me adjust from thinking about myself to being present for the other person. As the camera took a minute to come on, I took a deep breath.

Breathing is a common tactic we use to steady ourselves. Another tactic some people use is to put both feet under them flat on the ground. This can be particularly useful to prepare for conversations that are expected to be especially difficult, sensitive, or deep. It is a stabilizing physical position that can trigger being intentionally present.

I breathed a deep breath and planted my feet on the ground. The camera came on.

Marsha was visibly ... something. Was she agitated? Was she hurried? Was she angry or upset? It was not easily labeled, but something was not right.

Marsha started, "Hey Matt, how's it goin'?" she said, as almost a knee-jerk reaction as opposed to a genuine question.

"Busy day but doing good. How about you?" She seemed almost too distracted to answer my question. But after a deep sigh and a pause, she simply said, "Fine."

This was going to be a tough hour.

I said, "I don't know you well enough yet to say for sure, but you seem ... I don't know ... distracted?"

Marsha put down the paper she was holding and looked directly into the camera. You could tell she was filtering through the various ways she could respond and not finding the sentence she wanted.

After what seemed like the full hour we had scheduled, but likely just a few seconds, she finally said, "I have too much going on, and I'm not even prepared for this meeting." Marsha spoke with a manner of defeat. And I also sensed there was another emotion there that was just below the surface.

There are times in individual coaching, and it could probably be said for all verbal communication, when the best thing we can do for the conversation is to "let it breathe." Give a pause where every inclination is telling you to respond. Give space when answers or reactions seem so easy to find.

Fortunately, I was present enough at that moment to *not* respond — to not react. I maintained eye contact, my body was situated to be open and centered in front of the camera, and I leaned forward just slightly, to subtly indicate that I was fully engaged even if I wasn't saying anything.

She shifted uncomfortably in her seat.

"I am stressed and exhausted, and I don't see it ending. If I'm being honest with you, I'm not sure how much longer I can live this way."

Marsha was similar, in some ways, to many of the clients I've been introduced to over the past few years. Successful, driven, high-capacity, and carrying a heavy load. She also had primary caregiving duties for her two small children. Her husband also had a high-pressure, full-time role. But unlike her, he was not always the best at prioritizing anything other than his work. (As I would come to learn over the course of our eighteen months together, her husband had many shortcomings. The objectives of our work together did not include fixing her home life. Yet, as you can imagine, home life spills into work life and work life into home life.)

I paused again without responding. This time, there was a longer delay before her next words. After maybe two minutes of sitting in silence, she emptied many of her concerns over about twenty minutes of uninterrupted sharing.

As she did, I was completely focused on her. Not only did I want to make sure that I heard and comprehended as much as possible, but I also wanted to observe what was *not* said. I wanted to see her body language as she said certain things. I wanted to find those times when she repeated words or phrases or when she put a special emphasis on a word or a point.

Put yourself in this moment. What is it like to be fully present at this point in a conversation? Fortunately, I was.

She shared frustrations about the demands of her role. "My boss, my peers, the dozens of stakeholders I interact with ... They're all asking so much of me. It's just too much."

She vented about the lack of clarity and direction she received from her boss. "She thinks she's being clear when she tells me to do something, but she's not. She gives me very little to go on, and then she's critical when I don't give her what she wants. Sometimes, she'll completely change the request in the middle of the process. All of this creates so much extra work for me and oftentimes my team!"

She tearfully admitted the struggles that she was facing at home and how that was interfering with her day-to-day. "My spouse is starting to lose his patience with the amount of work I'm bringing home. It isn't fair to my family, but I have to get it done some time."

Eventually, she came to a place in her sharing where she paused and tried to make a joke. "Outside of that, I'm doing pretty well!" she quipped.

I smiled and prepared to respond. As you can imagine, at that moment, I was praying for the right words to say or the best question to ask. I think I was granted something close to good.

"Thank you for sharing, Marsha. First, thank you for trusting me with your concerns. I appreciate you bringing this to our time together."

She nodded affirmatively.

"What does it feel like to share what you shared?"

She thought about it. "I guess it's just nice to say it out loud. I don't have a lot of safe places where I can say some of these things."

Again, I paused.

She continued, "It's just that I'm not any closer to figuring any of this out."

I nodded. "You shared a number of different areas of concern. Of those, what would you say is most urgent or pressing?"

She responded, "Well, this meeting that I'm leading later tomorrow is probably the thing that feels particularly time-sensitive. I'm nervous about the potential conflict we may have in that meeting if I can't somehow convince a few of the stakeholders to come with an open mind."

"Good," I said. "That sounds like a good place to start."

We spent the rest of the hour talking through that specific situation, and she came away with a couple of actions she could take that made her feel a bit better equipped. We didn't solve all her concerns that day. But it did serve as a pivotal point for our work together over the coming year.

WHAT IF I WASN'T PRESENT?

Now imagine that scenario if I'd been unable or unwilling to reset myself and focus on being present. I had no idea what was coming, nor how it would turn out. But, because I was able to fully immerse myself in the conversation, I was able to help her navigate through a flood of issues and concerns. My ability to be present directly and positively impacted her day and week. Because I could center myself appropriately, I showed up the way she needed, when she needed it.

This is the epitome of what was discussed in Chapter 3 (Coaching Habit #1 – Focusing on Others). It's about being what others need you to be. It starts with the belief that you are capable of it, the one being coached is worth it, and you are committed to that behavior.

CHAPTER 8

COACHING HABIT #6
DRIVING RESULTS

Habit Is Seen As: Results-Oriented
Value or Belief Behind This Habit: It's About You Too

NARRATIVE

If you have been a part of my team for any period of time or I've worked with you in a mentoring situation, you're likely sick of me talking about "narrative."

Let's unpack that word narrative:

- a spoken or written account of connected events; a story:
  - "the hero of his modest narrative"
- the narrated part or parts of a literary work, as distinct from dialogue:
  - "the dialogue and the narrative suffer from awkward syntax"

- the practice or art of telling stories:
  - "traditions of oral narrative"
- a representation of a particular situation or process in such a way as to reflect or conform to an overarching set of aims or values:
  - "the coalition's carefully constructed narrative about its sensitivity to recession victims"[10]

In the context of coaching, we often explore the narratives that we use with others and, most often, the narratives we tell ourselves.

Energy Leadership Index is a powerful example of an assessment that is meant to help you better understand your internal narratives. Once you can name them and then identify them when they show up, you have the ability to adjust or replace those narratives with something that serves you better.

Some examples:

- "I keep hearing 'no' over and over and over again" could turn into, "I'm excited about experiencing my next 'yes.'"
- "I'm so busy, I'm so busy, I'm too busy," could become, "I can prioritize; I am capable."
- "God, I'm exhausted!" might be replaced by a completely unrelated thought like, "I'm looking forward to lunch with John tomorrow!"

The more I learn about and coach people through potentially harmful narratives, the more I've come to understand my own internal repetitive thoughts that don't always serve me well.

WHAT'S YOUR EXTERNAL NARRATIVE?

In people development, the narratives we use to describe ourselves externally are very important, too.

As an example, we're prone to think that good work is observable and that people are paying attention. There are many people who have some combination of these opinions. They think and/or say out loud:

> *"I work hard and do my job well. My work speaks for itself."*

No, it doesn't. Our work doesn't have a voice. We give it voice — if we choose to do so.

Or this:

> *"I just do my job. I'm not the kind of person who goes around bragging about myself."*

That's a thought often based in humility and a strong work ethic. Unfortunately, your work still risks not being seen and not being recognized.

Or:

> *"I'm not looking to get promoted right now. I'm satisfied with my current role."*

Awesome, except you are still subject to performance reviews, manager evaluations, and/or peer reviews. You're probably still interested in being considered for important projects or responsibilities. You remain concerned about your wages and the potential to increase them through a raise or a merit increase.

Which of these thoughts can you identify with, or which have you seen in others?

The reality is that your work is a vital piece of the objectives of the organization or entity that employs you. They expect what you do to lead to an outcome that involves a return on their investment in you. That might be higher revenue, more efficiencies, better consumer ratings, future innovation, or a multitude of other ways to produce value for them.

If we accept that premise, then it follows suit that part of our responsibility in that arrangement is to provide our employer ample access to the data or clues that suggest those things are happening.

How you share, with what frequency, and what you include is always negotiable. Regardless of your personality style, you can have success in this area. Let's develop a communication strategy for you to "prove your worth."

You are invited to use this series of questions to determine how you can best share your narrative in a way that feels authentic to you. (If you'd like a downloadable worksheet for this exercise, please visit *mattdickersonvalued.com.*)

- What have I done recently that I am particularly proud of? Or, what do I feel like I do really well (or might potentially enjoy doing)?
  - Answering this question will get this process started in an area that you have some attraction to or an affinity for.

- In what ways does that align with the objectives or goals of those in my sphere of influence? My business unit? My company?
  - With this answer, you hope to discover the overlap (picture a Venn diagram) where what you are good at also serves the company's best interest.
- What part of that do I feel comfortable sharing? With whom should I share it?
  - With the first question, you are creating boundaries for yourself, especially if you can relate to some of the examples of the narrative statements above. If you prefer to keep to yourself, you are likely motivated to set these kinds of boundaries.
  - For the second question, you might consider:
    - Cultural norms: How is this type of news typically shared?
    - Potential advocates: Who would *you* most like to tell about your accomplishments? Who could help you advance some of your career goals if they knew a bit more about what you're doing?
    - Interested parties: Who would *want* to hear about this tactic? Maybe you're doing something that confirms something someone else is doing. In a sales and marketing organization, for example, marketing spends a lot of resources on developing tools and messaging for sales to use. If you're having success in sales as a result of one of their tools, they're going to want to hear about it! We'll explore this more later in this chapter when I discuss the practice of

> implementing marketing tactics immediately after being trained on them.

- What is your preferred method of communication?
  - Would it be easier for you to take your time crafting an email that says exactly what you want to say?
  - Or would you prefer to give someone a quick call and chat about it?

Using this kind of evaluation in your communication strategy allows you to control a lot of the process and offers you the chance to build your narrative on your terms. This is the area of development that really requires the individual to be proactive, not waiting on their leader to take the initiative.

In a company of any size or industry, there are things the company or your leaders in a subset of the company want or need to prioritize. They have goals and expectations. They have deliverables and a pecking order of what needs to be accomplished and what can wait.

One of the easiest ways to ingratiate yourself with leaders in your company is to care about what they care about.

One of the easiest ways to ingratiate yourself with leaders in your company is to care about what they care about.

A good example of this dynamic can be found in national sales meetings many companies conduct several times a year. Sales, marketing, and the training department gather for new direction on the products they're selling at the time. Marketing does a ton of research and develops a strategy for the go-to-market activities. Marketing advises training on their objectives, and training's responsibility is to deliver training for the salespeople that meets those objectives.

As you might imagine, marketing is *very* interested in the sales experience in the weeks immediately following this training. If you find yourself in this situation, one way you can keep yourself on others' radar is to be deliberate about (1) trying out the things you were trained on and (2) reporting back your experience or newfound ideas, especially if you were able to achieve a new success using these new tools or tactics. There are a lot of people in this situation who are looking to prove that all their effort was worth it.

This is what building a narrative for yourself looks like. It is a story of a collaborator and someone willing and able to follow and execute the direction given. You are aiming to be seen as results-oriented.

 ## COACHING HABIT #6 – DRIVING RESULTS

HABIT IS SEEN AS: RESULTS-ORIENTED
VALUE OR BELIEF BEHIND THIS HABIT: IT'S ABOUT YOU TOO

Coaching others has allowed me a view into a level of leadership (at least by title) much higher than my professional career has taken me. I have sat with leader after leader and have seen some common themes.

WHERE'S THE RETURN ON INVESTMENT (ROI)?

One theme is that some in formal leadership don't have a passion for or a desire to develop others. Some say they're interested in mentoring and coaching, but the stories and issues they bring to our sessions rarely mention it. Sometimes, they make the outright claim that individuals are responsible for their own development and their role as leaders is more passive or reactive.

In those situations, leaders doubt the importance of investing in others. They often refer to it as something they'd do "if they had more time." If it's even on their radar, it is often deprioritized or overlooked.

Part of this is that they undervalue what might result from that investment of time. Any time they spend coaching is time away from strategy or vision or upholding the mission of the organization. There is limited return on investment, and therefore, it should be deprioritized. They have a duty to focus on the *most* important things for the company.

When their priorities influence the priorities of those who report to them, as they always do, there becomes a broad cultural disengagement from developing others, and middle managers and their reports suffer.

Yet, driving results for an organization cannot happen in a vacuum. All members of the team should be operating at their highest abilities in order to achieve maximum results. Upskilling others is what produces exponential growth for the group and the broader organization.

Hopefully, at this point in the book, you have grown in your appreciation of what people leadership could be — what it could mean to others and how it could positively impact you, too.

You also have some tangible examples of people leadership bringing value to the company in the form of succession planning, among other areas.

You now know, if you didn't already, that you can't measure results simply by what you see in a spreadsheet or an earnings report.

As we discussed in Chapter 6 (Coaching Habit #4 – Modeling Growth), the core belief is that *you do not have to do it alone.* Your work can be exponential if you start the cycle of people investment with your team. Once equipped, your team can better align with and support your vision of success going forward. And if those equipped employees are retained within the organization, the things they learn in their development will reap rewards for the company for years to come.

A common example of this, used in many books, is the lemonade stand. A kid starts a lemonade stand that experiences some success. Once she's able to confirm that there's a market for what she sells, she has to weigh the benefits and risks of bringing on other stands and employees. She must do the math of how much time she'll miss selling if she has to spend it training others, buying supplies, and getting the stands set up. Ultimately, most stories draw the same conclusion.

Investing in others creates more revenue in the long term despite being a short-term drain on revenue or efficiencies.

I love the example of the lemonade stand because it puts some numbers (however contrived they might be for a hypothetical lemonade stand) to this theory that developing others has a return on investment that you can measure.

In another example, Gartner Sales Research found some interesting results when it came to the importance of coaching on sales performance. The upshot of their research was summarized like this:[11]

> "Frontline sales staff reporting they receive **effective coaching** achieve **19% higher percent to goal** than their peers."

Both the story of the lemonade stand and this research from Gartner convey the importance of spending time helping others get better.

Unfortunately, the impact of coaching and mentoring is not always apparent. If the return on investment is proven, it is frequently many weeks or months later, and participants in this scenario might risk not linking the action (coaching) to the result (progress, sales, efficiency, etc.).

All of that said, there seems to be a shift in thinking in the workplace. Some might attribute it to ever-evolving professional development and companies' focus on delivering content and material that support individual growth.

The company I currently work for is seemingly always updating the training options we have. And as noted earlier in the book, I've been the beneficiary of many on-the-job upskill opportunities in various areas of the company. These opportunities do not come about without planning and dedicated resources organized by employees of the company.

To state it clearly: Attracting, leading, developing, training, retaining, and advancing talent have positive ROI for an organization.

> Attracting, leading, developing, training, retaining, and advancing talent have positive ROI for an organization.

WHAT EXAMPLES HAVE WE ALREADY COVERED?

You could point to the example of Trent in Chapter 1 (What is Leadership?). He was promoted to two account management positions in two other geographies, filling holes the company would have otherwise had to fill with a potentially less-qualified internal candidate or an external replacement. He was a great success for many years in those roles.

Or we could go back to Aisha's story in Chapter 5 (Value or Belief Behind This Habit – You Facilitate Their Growth). She was the employee who conducted back-to-back part-time roles while still maintaining individual success in her full-time sales territory. She accomplished the completion of projects, the introduction of standards and processes, and other work that will benefit the company for years to come. And now, she's taking all that knowledge and skill and is part of starting up a brand new sales force in another business unit.

Or we could revisit the story of Jan and Edward, also in Chapter 5. The company was at risk of losing a valuable member of the team or, maybe worse yet, having a team member who was less than engaged and enthusiastic. Because Jan had coaching and she used elevated skills to relate to her employee, Edward was retained and is more likely to stay.

Leading people well is done by coaching effectively. Coaching effectively, in the context of formal people leadership, is always results-oriented.

COACHING HABIT #6 – DRIVING RESULTS

HABIT IS SEEN AS: RESULTS-ORIENTED
VALUE OR BELIEF BEHIND THIS HABIT: IT'S ABOUT YOU TOO

In Chapter 6 (Coaching Habit #4 – Modeling Growth), I discussed how my team and their commitment to the support of others allows me to take some chances on the level of experience I look for when I'm hiring.

This dynamic allows me to hire candidates that I have reason to believe have great capacity beyond an average sales representative — whether that's consistent growth toward excelling in their current role or being part of a pipeline of talent for the broader organization.

I've had my ups and downs as a people manager. Perhaps my most consistent and widely agreed upon strength is my ability to develop talented people for the benefit of the organization.

Coaching habits have built and sustained whatever success I have achieved.

It's about me, too.

Investing in others and their professional development serves a purpose for you.

It's about you, too.

REALLY INVESTING IN PEOPLE

To protect the actors in this story, I'll take some liberties with the details. However, the outcome is real, and the moral is important.

Many years back, my company had a department that focused on hiring those with little or no sales experience for entry-level sales positions. They were frequently young or at least early in their professional careers.

Their charge was to cover vacant sales territories by phone. These vacancies could be the result of someone taking a rotation in another department with plans to return to the role, a salesperson taking long-term leave, or someone leaving the company altogether.

Some of the most fulfilling mentoring and coaching experiences of my career to date have taken place in my many years of supporting that department.

I also took on some tough cases.

One team member was about six months into her career when we started working together. She was not progressing well in her development and had fallen significantly behind her peers in performance.

Worse yet, there was a common concern among sales leadership that she wasn't appropriately engaged in her own development. Many feared it wouldn't work out.

I had an open territory in my division at the time, and I had a history of taking candidates in what we knew would be temporary assignments. Some leaders shied away from subjecting their customers to a revolving door of partners with our company, but I thought it was manageable and worth the risk.

These candidates often asked questions that sparked our own curiosity. They were a breath of fresh air for an experienced team.

They also provided ample opportunities for leaders on my team to step into mentoring and coaching. I give some credit to the early days of this program and my adoption of it in my division to the culture of growth and development on my team for years to come.

I thought I was inheriting a mess. What I got was a misunderstood and under-supported "diamond in the rough." She was, let's say, quirky for sure. And ... she was well-traveled, highly intelligent, and, most important to me, willing to learn.

The short and protected version was that the leader she went to work for had only been in the role a short time. The team did not have a culture of support and assistance, and she struggled to adapt to a role in which she had no experience.

I spent a lot of time with her and quickly discovered that she could be developed. The details of this transformation might be saved for a future writing because her growth and eventual success aren't the point of this story.

She successfully grew in her sales execution and interviewed well for a permanent sales position in another area of the country. She went on to have several successful years in that territory until she left for a better opportunity outside of the company.

The moral of this story is that it pays to invest in people. The company was able to fill an important position by retaining a valuable employee in the process.

CHAPTER 9

CLOSING THOUGHTS

My most important work is the last thing I did.
— **Mary Beth Edelson**

This book provides you with a practical framework for what actual investment into people looks like. It's one thing to say, "I buy the idea, but what can I do to take a step toward what you describe?" It's quite another to feel like you're equipped to take up that charge and pursue leading well.

THE SIX COACHING HABITS

The six coaching habits are built to provide a logical path by which you can grow into your role or in preparation for your future role. While they are linear in their most basic adoption, growth is messy. You will jump from habit to habit in the moment and over time as the situation and your ability to address it fluctuate. That's not only okay but expected.

You start by *focusing on others* — you embody an other-focused mentality. By asking good questions and being different for different people, you are "easy to work with" instead of working in support of objectives that don't just meet your needs.

You then can move into growing in your skill to *recognize what's needed of you*. Through a better understanding of each team member's personality and tendencies, you begin to adapt your behavior to show up in a way that they value and appreciate. This doesn't necessarily have to come naturally to you. As in my example, your alignment to your core values or your general satisfaction might make investing in others an energy booster as opposed to an energy exhauster.

Once you understand your *humble confidence*, you can move into a rigor of *being intentionally proactive*. You can take ownership of your role in others' development and understand that your proactivity is not only an opportunity but a requirement of leading people well. You have come to clarity on the responsibility of the individual in comparison to the accountability all people leaders should be held to.

Since you have gained knowledge of others and their tendencies, you can refocus on yourself. How can you *model growth* in a way that is both inspiring and sets the standards or the tone for the group or team? You come to realize that your actions in your own self-development directly impact your team's views on their own stretch assignments. Your modeling provides them a "cheat sheet" of what to do when giving their time and energy to others.

You have come to an understanding that true growth cannot come without *reflection and acknowledgement*. You give space for you and those around you to process news at their own pace, and you leave room for open dialogue. You create an environment that is undeniably inclusive and understanding. You learn that your presence is not just your physical representation in the room but also your whole self engaged in the moment and attentive to the needs of others.

And finally, you come back to where you started in some sense. You focus on the return on investment and what's in it for you. *But* your views of what this is and how it might be accomplished have been greatly expanded. You now know that true corporate growth is intertwined with individuals' needs to be taken care of professionally and emotionally.

You now know why this is important and how to build an action plan to develop toward being this ideal leader.

FINDING YOUR WHY

My hope is that you have also uncovered why this is important *to you*. What points resonate the most with you? What are your core values, and how do they intersect with what you've learned here? Are you in a position now to reevaluate your stance on people leadership and the role it plays in your life and your career?

I've had some of the thoughts in this book floating around in my head for years; others, I've only recently discovered.

What's more, over the course of time, I've changed my mind about a lot.

In Chapter 4, I mentioned one of my favorite podcasts, *Coaching for Leaders*, with Dave Stachowiak.

Frequently, at the end of an episode, he asks the guest some form of, "What have you recently changed your mind about?"

I love this part of the podcast! His guests have such interesting stories in their responses. There's a lot of value in what he shares with the world, and that part of his show is among them.

I've changed much about my approach and my intentions. What I haven't changed my mind about is how important people development is in leading people well.

As I was writing this book, one word kept coming to me: Valued.

It came up in my personal need to be valued. At the intersection of two of my three core values, belonging and achievement, I need to feel like I am being valued for what I bring to the table.

It is the root of "valuable," which is what the company expects its employees to be. Driving results, attracting and retaining talent, and executing my role expectations are ways in which I prove that I am valuable to the company and to those who rely on my support.

Core values, such as the two of mine I just listed, are the basis of every decision we make, whether we know it or not. Once we have some idea about what is *most* important to us, we have the strength and clarity of thought to move decisively and say no to things that don't align with what is core to us.

At its most basic, I hope that I have provided *value* to you, the reader, in what I shared here.

Most importantly, though, I wrote this with the heart for everyone who seeks professional fulfillment — satisfaction in what they do at work, whatever that might be.

I had an amazing travel experience recently that I've shared broadly within my organization.

I was in a season of heavy travel and found myself in my third hotel in as many nights. I was desperate to print something, and at each stop, there was a reason I couldn't. In one, the computers were down. In another, the printer wasn't properly connected. And in the third, the front desk person admitted that she didn't think the printers had *ever* worked at their location.

I was feeling the pressure of the road and being away from my family. And I was just plain mad that I couldn't get what I wanted (I'm not particularly proud of this).

Over the phone from my room, the front desk person offered the option of emailing my document to her, and she would print it at her station. I fumed all the way down in the elevator after sending the much-needed email. As I exited the elevator, I was confronted with an immovable thought: "Calm down." What can I say? It was a God moment.

I rounded the corner to find two employees at the front desk. When I said I was the one who had phoned, the woman I'd been speaking to immediately began the process of printing what I needed. The other engaged me in conversation. I shared that I was on the road and finding printing services hard to come by. She asked me what I did, and I shared that I managed a team that sold vaccines.

"In fact," I said, feeling a little bit more conversant and less angry, "we just got licensure for a product that prevents against RSV disease in infants." Respiratory syncytial virus is the leading cause of hospitalizations in infants, and there has never been a way to prevent this disease that was available to all infants.

The second employee, the one not wrestling with the printer, her whole demeanor changed. She said, "Well, now you're speaking my language."

She got out of her chair, walked around the counter, and stood about a foot from me. She carefully lifted the amulet of the necklace around her neck to reveal a picture of a young girl.

"This is my daughter, Leticia. She passed away when she was five years old from complications with asthma. We believe that her struggle started when she contracted severe RSV when she was not even one year old. If your medicine was available then, she might still be here."

Whoa. I was not ready for that. Fortunately, I had the peace of mind to comment on her daughter's beautiful name and thank her for sharing Leticia's story.

She said thanks for the work we do, and I made some comment deflecting to my team members and others like them around the country who actually had the hard job of making this immunization a part of what providers in their area offered.

I collected my paper, almost completely insignificant at this point, and said thanks. As I headed toward the elevator, floored at the unbelievable moment I had just experienced and thankful for my response in the midst of it, she said something behind me.

"Don't forget; what you do matters."

Everyone deserves to feel *valued*.

You deserve to feel *valued*.

You can find fulfillment through helping others find their *value*.

Leading others could be the way you find *value* in your career.

If you are fortunate enough to have the opportunity to help others grow, please remember:

What you do matters!

ENDNOTES

1   Ruchika Tulshyan: *Inclusion on Purpose: An Intersectional Approach to Creating a Culture of Belonging at Work* (Cambridge: The MIT Press, 2022), 10.

2   Used with permission – Rachel Pritz – https://www.rachelpritz.com

3   Visit mattdickersonvalued.com for more information on personality assessment comparisons, information, and links.

4   *(Note: These questions were adapted from various personality assessment platforms I have worked with.)*

5   Jerry Toomer, Craig Caldwell, Steve Weitzenkorn, and Chelsea Clark: *The Catalyst Effect* (Bingley: Emerald Publishing, 2018), 123.

6   Please visit mattdickersonvalued.com for examples of reflection questions and guides to better reflection.

7   *(This model builds on several like models. For example, many guides on emotional intelligence promote that we pause, assess, and respond (PAR), or assess, pause, and respond (APR). The Cleveland Consulting Group uses PRC (pause, reflect, and choose). While these models are valuable, including all four of the steps espoused here is critical to being actively engaged.)*

8   Kevin Cashman: *The Pause Principle* (San Fransisco: Berrett-Koehler Publishers, 2012), 57.

9   Energy Leadership Index: https://www.energyleader-ship.com/assessment, Positive Intelligence: https://www.positiveintelligence.com

10 *Oxford Languages (via Google)*, s.v. "narrative (n.)," accessed October 11, 2023, https://www.google.com/search?q=narrative

11 Gartner, Inc., 2020.

ACKNOWLEDGEMENTS

I would like to first thank God for the amazing gift of life that he has given me. Among other ways I think He powers my life, I can't count the number of times I have been in a coaching situation or a moment of people leadership when I came up with what appeared to be the right choice for my response. In those moments, I know that I did not power that answer. I was not prepared of my own volition. He gave me the words or the reaction or the action that the other person needed in that moment. Among the many gifts He gives me, I thank Him for that in this context.

I am so thankful for my life partner and best friend, Carrie. She is my wife of more than twenty years. She is my great equalizer. She balances me when I get out of balance (which happens more than it should). She is a constant in the lives of our daughters, much to their benefit. She puts up with me and my crazy ideas — this book is a great example.

We are partners in everything, and I could not have chosen a better person to link with forever.

My two daughters, Abby and Lily, have had to endure similar dad dreams and have never been anything but supportive. They are excited about this book for me, and I have felt their support throughout the book writing process. They are huge successes in their own rights, and I am so excited for what God has in store for them.

Thank you to my parents, Gene and Frances, for providing me with a strong foundation and daily glimpses of what a successful partnership looks like.

A special thank you to my only sibling, my sister Becky. We probably don't talk about it enough, but you are an inspiration to me. Your single-mindedness and your passion for what you do for a living are a North Star for what I am trying to build in my own life. You paved the way for something like a published book to even be a consideration. You produced a fundamentally strong resource for parents of young children, and it is just one way in which I am proud to be your brother.

Thank you also to the many other contributors to this book. I appreciate those who took the time to fill out my survey. Your feedback and stories made this book better. A special thanks to Rachel Pritz for her Enneagram expertise and valuable content. Thank you to Mike McGinley, who not only offered content for this book but has also been an amazing mentor and friend for many years. Some of my favorite development conversations have come in his company.

I am blessed to be tied to many great people at The Catalyst Effect. Jerry Toomer and Courtney Salati have placed great trust in me over the past few years. It is hard to put into words how important their endorsement of me has been. I am lucky to be in their circle. A special thanks to Jerry for his foreword and his mentoring through this writing process.

A huge thanks to the Niche Pressworks team and their amazing collection of coaches, editors, designs, and advisors that helped me curate my ideas and expertise into a book I am excited to share with the world. Nicole Gebhardt and

Linda Dessau, in particular, thank you for your help with the content and clarity of my message; and Kim Han for your guidance and encouragement through every step. I shudder to think what this book would have been without such amazing guidance and coaching. Your team changed the course of my writing and publishing journey in such positive ways. Thank you.

I have so many people to thank for my professional development. I fear I will inevitably miss someone. Thank you to my leaders, who were strong examples of many of the ideas I share here. Mike Stilwell, Mike Schmidt, Jeff Austin, Mike Gruetzmacher, Brad Bracken, Laura Grandis — your leadership examples were not necessarily perfect but always heartfelt and committed to my betterment.

I'd like to thank those who have been involved in my development less directly. This is where I will certainly miss someone important. Thank you to Mary Ann and Angie, who taught me early what sacrificial leadership might look like. Thank you to my early peer leaders who fed into me in the midst of my naivety despite not having a direct-report relationship. Thank you to Patrick Engkjer, Tom Hodar, Doug Detweiler, Jen Maguire, Nicole Wilson, and Bobby Grzenda for your mentorship and guidance.

A special thank you to two brothers who have been an integral part of my success for well over a decade — Rafael Melendez and Bill Spurlock. Our relationship means more to me than you can know. As I point out in the book, your ability to be exceptional at what you do allowed me to take many of the chances that I did.

I want to take this opportunity to thank those who directly contributed to my consideration and my selection in the coaching program. I had no idea what it was or how I might be right for it and it for me. But you all had some faith I was on the right track. Thank you to Tony Primerano, Mimi Doherty, Deb Lewandowski, Isabelle Aubin, Bill Ahern, and Christine Vaccola.

Thank you to Kaveh Naficy and Chris Brookfield for providing an amazing coach training experience. The skills you taught and the heart you transferred to me resonate in my work today, several years later.

I would like to extend my sincerest thanks to the many who have allowed me to be a part of their development. Whether it was for a short season or over a long period of time, you trusted me to be a part of your journey. I am honored by anyone who invites me in and allows me to align my core values with what I do professionally.

ABOUT MATTHEW J. DICKERSON

Matt believes that all good leaders encounter times in their careers when they cannot find answers on their own. He is convinced that his purpose in life is to help people through those moments.

Matt has enjoyed a twenty-year career in sales and management that serves as the foundation of his skills for coaching and mentoring. He has worked in multiple industries, with the majority of his experience in pharmaceuticals/vaccines.

During his time with a global pharmaceutical company, Matt was instrumental in developing and executing new tools for people development. He coached coaches on how to be more effective people developers and managers. He also created a curriculum that supported skill growth in coaching for performance.

Matt has a bachelor's degree in political science from Purdue University and a master's in business administration from the University of Indianapolis. He is recognized as a professional certified coach (PCC) through the International Coaching Federation (ICF). He is the former board president of Family Promise of Greater Indianapolis and the current president of the Indiana chapter of ICF.

He enjoys spending time with his wife and two teen daughters and working in his recently built workshop. He's a lover of music and an avid reader. To stay active, he plays tennis and runs (although not as often as he should).

> *"At the heart of coaching is the assertion that everyone has their own truth and the skills with which to navigate life — professional and personal. All team members have leadership capabilities and deserve to be developed and nurtured."*
> — **Matthew J. Dickerson**

CONTACT

Website: mattdickersonvalued.com

Email: matt@mattdickersonvalued.com

LinkedIn: linkedin.com/in/matt-dickerson-6008b1b